The Diabetes Holiday Cookbook

Year-Round Cooking for People with Diabetes

Carolyn Leontos, M.S., R.D., C.D.E.
Debra Mitchell, C.E.P.C.
Kenneth Weicker, C.E.C.

John Wiley & Sons, Inc.

Published by John Wiley & Sons, Inc., New York
Published simultaneously in Canada

This publication is designed to provide accurate and authoritative information in regard to the subject
matter covered. It is sold with the understanding that the publisher is not engaged in rendering
professional services. If professional advice or other expert assistance is required, the services of a
competent professional person should be sought.

Library of Congress Cataloging-in-Publication Data

Leontos, Carolyn.
The diabetes holiday cookbook : year-round cooking for people with diabetes /
Carolyn Leontos, Debra Mitchell, Kenneth Weicker.
p.   cm.
Includes bibliographical references and index.
ISBN 0-471-02805-3
1. Diabetes—Diet therapy—Recipes.   2. Holiday cookery.
I. Mitchell, Debra.   II. Weicker, Kenneth.   III. Title.
RC662 .L464   2002
616.4'620654—dc21   2001007724

Printed in the United States of America

10   9   8   7   6   5   4   3   2   1

Contents

Foreword

It may take a village to help raise a family, but if that family includes a person with diabetes, it takes just one special villager, such as Carolyn Leontos, to show them the way to a long, healthy life.

As a registered dietitian and a certified diabetes educator, Carolyn Leontos has affected the lives of those with diabetes in the best way possible. Through her compassionate approach to problem-solving and her books and programs (too many to count!), she leads them to the dining room and makes them happy to be there.

We met many years ago and have worked together on many projects. Carolyn was a constant guest on my call-in radio show. As my nutrition and diabetes specialist, she was always available to spread the word about a healthy way of life. Her reassuring answers to callers, whose lives had changed when they or a family member was diagnosed with diabetes, are still remembered.

It wasn't only those who had diabetes that she educated. Carolyn entered the kitchens of every hotel in Las Vegas to spread the word about the need for healthier eating. Like the Pied Piper, Carolyn soon had the chefs following her lead. Two of them created the recipes for this important new book, *The Diabetes Holiday Cookbook.*

Certified Executive Chef Ken Weicker is the executive chef of the Suncoast Resort in Las Vegas; Certified Executive Pastry Chef Debra Mitchell is the executive pastry chef at Treasure Island, a Mirage/MGM Grand hotel. These talented chefs have created a collection of recipes and menus geared to holidays for every month of the year.

The scope of the recipes and menus shows just how far healthy eating limits can be stretched, even for people with diabetes. The only restriction now seems to be portion size! Although this book was written for those with diabetes, it could stand on its own as a delicious guide to a healthier way of eating for everyone, where little is forbidden—not even potato kugel (Passover), chicken enchiladas (Cinco de Mayo), roast rib of beef (Christmas), or delicious desserts!

Muriel Stevens
Food Editor, Restaurant Critic,
and Consumer Advocate
Las Vegas Sun
Las Vegas, Nevada

Acknowledgments

We want to thank: Art Leontos, whose inspiration, love, and support were the basis for this project; Fran and Ryan Weicker, who researched, typed, and tasted innumerable recipes; Jessica Tate, who kindly tasted many recipes lacking her favorite ingredient (sugar); Jesus Castillo, who also helped with research; and Elizabeth Zack, our editor, for her insightful comments that kept us on track and made this book easier to read.

Note: All recipes were analyzed using Nutritionist Five (nutrition software for recipe analysis), First Data Bank, San Bruno, California.

Introduction

The Diabetes Holiday Cookbook is written for everyone who is concerned about good health. It is for:

- every person who has diabetes—to help him or her cope with special occasions while still taking good care of themselves and maintaining good glucose control
- all the people who care about someone with diabetes
- every mother who has been frustrated while trying to plan a birthday party for her child with diabetes
- every spouse who wants to make a holiday special for a partner with diabetes
- every family member and every friend who wants to include a loved one who has diabetes in celebrations.

(And, in fact, anyone who cares about delicious, healthful eating can benefit from the information and recipes in this book!)

There have been many advances in the treatment of diabetes in recent years. We now know much more about how to manage this disease: we know that you can adjust insulin dosages to "cover" extra carbohydrates, thereby giving people with diabetes options to eat foods that were previously forbidden. That makes choosing foods for celebrations easier—but as is the case for everyone, taking in more calories than you use will result in unwanted weight gain.

This book takes you through the holidays month by month, starting with New Year's Day all the way to Christmas and Kwanzaa. For each you will find a little bit of history about each holiday, as well as menus with tested recipes and suggestions for appropriate, calorie-free ways to celebrate the day. Food is an important part of any celebration, so each holiday in this book has its own festive menu, complete with recipes. Some holiday menus are more elaborate and offer buffet-table selections. Others give you suggestions for the whole day—and you could even end up with leftovers, too! You may want to use the entire menu or select only one or two recipes to go with your favorites. Or you may want to mix and match to suit your own taste. The Roast Pork Loin we suggest for New Year's, for example, may be just what you want for Easter. Or our Thanksgiving turkey might be your Christmas entrée.

Keep in mind that the recipes are designed to be *festive*. Although added sugar and fat are kept to a minimum, these foods are not meant to be eaten every day. You'll find new and improved fat and sugar replacers offering many delicious options that were not possible even a few years ago. Some of these recipes also use alcohol as an ingredient, but in every case we have given you an alternative if you do not wish to use alcohol in your food preparation. As food safety is always a concern, be sure to use a meat thermometer to ensure that your entrées have reached a safe temperature.

Gourmet chefs Kenneth Weicker and Debra Mitchell will also reveal ways to enhance flavor while adding few or no calories. Lemon or orange zest—the grated rind of the fruit—can intensify citrus flavor without increasing carbohydrate. You will learn what to do with overripe bananas, even on a day when you don't have time to bake!

Some things to keep in mind: Use cooking spray, such as Pam, to prepare your baking pans. And always remove visible fat from meat and meat juice or broth. Every time you discard a tablespoon of fat, you are throwing away *120 calories!* Some recipes may have more sodium than you want to take in. Reduce the sodium by eliminating or cutting back on salt itself or on a salty ingredient. Capers, for example, are high in sodium and could be left out if sodium is a concern. Garlic is another "adjustable" ingredient. It is low in calories, fat, and sodium, so you can add more or cut back as your taste dictates. Whatever else you do, *do not eat anything unless you really enjoy the taste.* Our philosophy? A calorie is a terrible thing to waste, and you shouldn't squander it on anything that isn't high quality, truly delicious, and something you *really* enjoy.

Numerous advances in the treatment of diabetes over recent years have given people many more choices in what they eat. Nevertheless, it is important to remember that everyone with diabetes has individual needs, and not every recipe in this book may be appropriate for everyone. In general, however, the recipes are tasty, nutritious alternatives that may benefit anyone concerned about health and caloric intake. Still, if you have a question about any specific food, check with your doctor or dietitian. Calorie, carbohydrate, fat, and exchange information is included for each recipe, so that you or your doctor or dietitian can make appropriate choices.

Portion size is also an important issue. International travelers know that in the United States portions are larger than in other parts of the world. Generally speaking, most people, whether they have diabetes or not, would be better off with smaller portions. So if calories are a concern, think "international" when planning your parties. Think quality rather than quantity—and enjoy!

January

New Year's Day
Chinese New Year

New Year's Day

January 1

New Year's Day is one of the world's oldest holidays, originating from the time of the ancient Egyptians and Babylonians. Since the era of Julius Caesar it has been celebrated at the beginning of the year on January 1.

January was named after the Roman god Janus, who is depicted with two faces—one looking forward, the other backward. Likewise, as we celebrate the New Year, we celebrate also the triumphs and successes of the past year and look forward to what the coming year will bring.

Both New Year's Eve *and* New Year's Day are great times to have parties. It is a wonderful time of year to say good-bye to the old and welcome in the new with family and friends. The Tournament of Roses Parade is a long California tradition, and television has extended its reach throughout the country. The Rose Bowl, always an exciting college football game, follows it. Together they make a great excuse for a party!

Pennsylvania is home to another famous parade: the Mummers Parade, held in Philadelphia on New Year's Day. This tradition dates from the 1700s and has been officially sponsored by the city of Philadelphia since 1901. It is a celebration in which all the participants sport elaborate costumes (the word "mummer" means a person who wears a disguise or mask for fun).

Feasting on traditional New Year's foods is an international practice. In the southern part of the United States, black-eyed peas are eaten to ensure prosperity for the coming year. Some people eat leafy green vegetables such as cabbage (a slang term for paper money) to bring financial luck. In Spain, it is believed that eating twelve grapes brings good luck in the next twelve months, while in England a drink from the wassail bowl signifies a toast to good health.

If you are entertaining, plan your menu so that your guests have choices. If any of your guests have diabetes or some other reason to be concerned about what they eat, make sure you serve a variety of foods and include some yummy low-calorie treats. Good Luck Black-Eyed "Peas," which are sometimes known as cowpeas, are really beans. They are easy to recognize because of the dark dot on their cream-colored skin. They also are low in fat and a good source of carbohydrate, fiber, vitamins, and minerals. (With that résumé it is no surprise that they bring you good luck. But, most important, they taste great!)

This is a great time of year for new beginnings—that's why we have New Year's resolutions. Many people resolve to do things that will improve their lives, like exercising, losing weight, or saving money. Everyone knows that resolutions are much easier to make than to keep, but try to make healthful eating the whole year long one of your goals. Using this book you can celebrate the holidays with special foods all year long and *still* keep that resolution!

New Year's Day

Shrimp Cocktail

Julienne Vegetable Consommé

Roast Pork Loin with Mushroom Dressing

Good Luck Black-Eyed "Peas"

Chocolate "Bread" Pudding

or

Apple Crisp

Shrimp Cocktail

YIELD: 4 servings

1 tablespoon Old Bay Seasoning (or any shellfish seasoning)
½ small onion, thinly sliced
1 small carrot, sliced
1 stalk celery, chopped
1 lemon, cut in half

16 large or jumbo raw shrimp, shell on
Lettuce
8 tablespoons Cocktail Sauce (recipe follows)

In a pot with 4 cups of cold water, add the Old Bay, onion, carrot, celery, and lemon. Bring to a boil, turn the heat down, and simmer for 10 minutes. Add the shrimp and cook for 8 to 12 minutes (depending on size), counting from the time the water returns to a boil. The shrimp will be opaque and firm. Remove the shrimp and cover them with ice to cool quickly.

Discard the cooking liquid and vegetables. When the shrimp are cool enough to touch, peel off the shells. To devein, cut along the middle of the back from the head to the tail about ⅛ inch deep and pull out the dark vein. Rinse the deveined shrimp under cold water. Put a lettuce leaf on a plate or, if you prefer, chop lettuce and put it into a stemmed glass. Arrange four shrimp on plate or glass and drizzle 2 tablespoons Cocktail Sauce over shrimp.

Serving size: ¼ recipe	Calories from fat: 6	Sodium: 423 milligrams
Vegetable exchanges: 1	Total fat: 1 gram	Carbohydrate: 8 grams
Very-lean-meat	Saturated fat: 0 grams	Dietary fiber: 1 gram
exchanges: 1	Cholesterol: 43 milli-	Sugars: 4 grams
Calories: 60	grams	Protein: 6 grams

Cocktail Sauce

YIELD: 4 servings

4 tablespoons ketchup
3 tablespoons chili sauce
1 teaspoon lemon juice

1 teaspoon prepared horseradish (dry)
1 teaspoon caper juice*
½ teaspoon capers*, finely chopped

Mix all the ingredients.

Put the mixture in a clean, sanitized jar, cover, and refrigerate until ready to use. It will keep 2 weeks refrigerated.

Serving size: 2 table-	Total fat: 0 grams	Dietary fiber: 0 grams
spoons	Saturated fat: 0 grams	Sugars: 4 grams
Vegetable exchanges: 1	Cholesterol: 0 milligrams	Protein: 0 grams
Calories: 24	Sodium: 308 milligrams	
Calories from fat: 0	Carbohydrate: 6 grams	

*For lower sodium, omit capers and caper juice.

Julienne Vegetable Consommé

YIELD: 4 servings

2 medium ripe tomatoes
1 quart Vegetable Stock (recipe
   follows)
½ carrot, peeled

½ stalk celery
½ medium red pepper
½ medium green pepper
1 teaspoon chopped parsley

Wash the tomatoes and slice each one into about six pieces. Bring the vegetable stock to a simmer; add the tomatoes and continue to simmer for about 10 minutes. Strain the stock through a very fine strainer or coffee filter. Season to taste with salt and pepper.

Fill a medium-size pot with 2 cups of water and set it on medium-high heat. While waiting for the water to come to a boil, cut the carrot, celery, and peppers into fine julienne strips (1 inch long by ⅛ inch wide). Blanch the julienne (long, thin) vegetables in boiling water for 1 minute and drain. Divide the vegetables into 4 equal sections and put each section into one of 4 soup bowls. Top with the stock and sprinkle with the chopped parsley.

Serving size: 8 ounces	Total fat: 1 gram	Carbohydrate: 6 grams
Vegetable exchanges: 1	Saturated fat: 0 grams	Dietary fiber: 1 gram
Calories: 34	Cholesterol: 0 milligrams	Sugars: 3 grams
Calories from fat: 9	Sodium: 850 milligrams	Protein: 1 gram

Vegetable Stock

YIELD: 1½ quarts

4 stalks celery, leaves removed
3 large carrots, unpeeled
2 large yellow onions, unpeeled
½ head garlic, unpeeled
2 tablespoons parsley stems
1 tablespoon canola oil
2 teaspoons thyme

2 teaspoons marjoram
3 bay leaves
2 teaspoon black peppercorns,
   crushed
2 teaspoons salt (optional)
1 cup dry white wine (or water)
6 cups cold water

Wash all the vegetables and chop into ½-inch pieces. Place a 2-gallon pot on medium heat and add the oil. When the oil is hot, add all the vegetables carefully (as the oil may spatter) and lightly sauté over medium heat for 4 minutes, stirring from time to time. Do not brown. Add all the spices and stir.

Add the wine and simmer for 1 minute. Add the cold water and bring to a boil slowly over medium heat. Turn the heat down and lightly simmer for 60 minutes. Do not let the stock come to a rolling boil, or it may become cloudy. Strain through a large strainer or colander lined with a coffee filter or cheesecloth to remove all particles. This stock should be clear, with a slight golden hue and neutral flavor. You may use any vegetable in a stock. However, be aware that if strongly flavored vegetables are used, the stock will take on that flavor.

Note: Freeze any remaining vegetable stock in small containers for use in other recipes.

Serving size: 8 ounces	Total fat: 2 grams	Carbohydrate: 3 grams
Vegetable exchanges: 1	Saturated fat: 0 grams	Dietary fiber: 0 grams
Fat exchanges: ½	Cholesterol: 0 milligrams	Sugars: 1 gram
Calories: 39*	Sodium: 790 (15)[†] milli-	Protein: 0 grams
Calories from fat: 21	grams	Alcohol: 1 gram*

Roast Pork Loin with Mushroom Dressing

YIELD: 6 servings

2 pounds boneless center-cut pork loin
2 cloves fresh garlic, very finely chopped

1 teaspoon salt (optional)
2 teaspoons black pepper
1 teaspoon rosemary

*If you use water instead of wine, the stock will have 32 calories per serving and 0 grams of alcohol.

[†]Figure in parentheses does not include salt.

Preheat the oven to 350°.

Trim off all exterior fat from the pork loin. Combine the chopped garlic with salt, pepper, and rosemary. Rub the pork loin with this mixture to season. Place the pork loin in a shallow pan, add 1 cup of water, cover with aluminum foil, and place in the oven for about 40 minutes. Uncover. Increase the temperature to 400° and continue cooking until an internal temperature of 165° is reached (on a meat thermometer inserted into the very center of the roast), or approximately 30 minutes more.

Remove from the oven, let stand for 20 minutes, then slice and serve. Serve sliced atop Mushroom Dressing with Good Luck Black-Eyed "Peas" (recipes follow).

Serving size: 3 ounces	Total fat: 7 grams	Sodium: 332 (41)* milligrams
Lean meat exchanges: 3	Saturated fat: 3 grams	Protein: 32 grams
Calories: 172	Cholesterol: 62 milligrams	
Calories from fat: 61		

Mushroom Dressing

YIELD: 6 servings

4 cups dry bread cubes (use stale bread, cut into ½-inch cubes or purchased croutons)
8 ounces mushrooms, sliced
1 stalk celery, finely chopped
¼ cup finely chopped onion
1 clove garlic, minced

1 tablespoon vegetable oil
1¾ cups Chicken Stock or Vegetable Stock (see recipes, pp. 21 and 11)
¼ teaspoon salt (optional)
Scant teaspoon black pepper
¼ teaspoon dried thyme

Cut the stale bread into ½-inch cubes or use purchased croutons. Measure 4 cups and set aside. Sauté all the vegetables in a 2-quart nonstick pan with the vegetable oil over medium heat until softened. Add the stock and bring to a boil. Add the seasonings. Turn off the heat, add the bread cubes all at once, and stir until well mixed. Turn the heat back on to medium-high and, stirring constantly, cook for about 3 minutes more. If the dress-

*Figure in parentheses does not include salt.

ing is too dry, you may add more stock; if dressing is too moist for your taste, cook a little longer to make it drier.

Serving size: ½ cup	Total fat: 4 grams	Carbohydrate: 14 grams
Starch exchanges: 1	Saturated fat: 0 grams	Dietary fiber: 1 gram
Fat exchanges: ½	Cholesterol: 0 milligrams	Sugars: 2 grams
Calories: 108	Sodium: 456 (243)*	Protein: 5 grams
Calories from fat: 36	milligrams	

Good Luck Black-Eyed "Peas"

YIELD: 16 servings

1 pound black-eyed peas
4 ounces bacon, diced
½ medium onion, finely chopped
2 stalks celery, finely chopped
2 cloves garlic, peeled and chopped

1 bay leaf
1 teaspoon salt
½ teaspoon pepper
2 tablespoons minced fresh parsley
1 green onion

Rinse the peas, put them in a large container, cover with plenty of water, and soak them in the refrigerator overnight.

Heat the bacon in a large pot over medium-low heat. When the bacon is slightly brown, add onion, celery, and garlic. Increase heat to medium high and sauté for two minutes. Add the bay leaf.

Drain the peas and add them to the pot. Add water to a level about 2 inches above the peas. Bring to a boil, reduce heat to simmer, and cook for 1 to 1½ hours, or until the peas are tender. Stir often, as the peas may stick. Remove and discard bay leaf. Take out about a third of the peas, put into the blender, and puree. Pour back into the remaining peas (this will thicken

*Figure in parentheses does not include salt.

the mixture). Add salt and pepper to taste. Mince the parsley and green onion and sprinkle on top just before serving.

Serving size: ¾ cup	Total fat: 3 grams	Dietary fiber: 3 grams
Starch exchanges: 1	Saturated fat: 1 gram	Sugars: 0 grams
Lean-meat exchanges: 1	Cholesterol: 8 milligrams	Protein: 9 grams
Calories: 134	Sodium: 301 milligrams*	
Calories from fat: 30	Carbohydrate: 18 grams	

Chocolate "Bread" Pudding

YIELD: 1 8-by-12-inch cake

Chocolate Chiffon Cake

⅞ cups cake flour
½ cup plus 2 tablespoons Splenda (sugar substitute)
1 teaspoon baking powder
¼ teaspoon salt
¼ cup cocoa powder
3 ounces boiling water

¼ cup oil
3 egg yolks
1 teaspoon vanilla extract
5 egg whites
½ teaspoon cream of tartar
¼ cup semisweet mini chocolate chips

Preheat the oven to 325°.

Sift together flour, ½ cup Splenda, baking powder, and salt. Place in the bowl of an electric mixer fitted with the paddle attachment. Make a well in the center of the dry ingredients. Mix the cocoa and boiling water, add to the well in the dry ingredients along with the oil, egg yolks, and vanilla, and beat until smooth.

In a separate bowl, whip the egg whites and cream of tartar and 2 tablespoons of Splenda to make a meringue. Whip until the egg whites form a stiff peak. Take a third of the flour mixture and gently fold into the meringue. Then fold the meringue back into the flour mixture. Fold in the chocolate chips. Pour into an 8-by-8-inch pan lightly coated with cooking

*This recipe is not recommended for low-sodium diets.

spray. Bake for 20 to 25 minutes. Cake should be lightly browned and spring back to touch. Allow to cool 30 minutes, then remove from pan.

Bread Pudding

4 cups 2% milk
6 eggs
¾ cup Splenda (sugar substitute)
6 ounces semisweet baking chocolate, melted

Chocolate Chiffon Cake, cut into ½-inch cubes. (You can bake the cake the day before if you wish.)
Sugar-free chocolate sauce (optional)

Preheat the oven to 300°.

Place the milk in a heavy saucepan over medium heat and bring to a boil. Remove from the heat. In a medium-size bowl, whisk together the eggs and Splenda. Slowly whisk the hot milk into the eggs. Whisk in the melted chocolate. Mix to combine completely.

Place the cake cubes evenly in the 8-by-12-inch baking dish, and pour the chocolate mixture over the cubes. Press the cubes down into the mixture to saturate them. Allow the pan to sit for 10 minutes, occasionally pressing the cubes into the liquid. Cover the pan with foil and place it on a cookie sheet in the preheated oven. Then carefully fill the cookie sheet with water. Bake approximately 1 hour and 25 to 30 minutes or until a knife inserted into the middle of the pan comes out clean. Cool about 10 minutes before serving. Cut into squares and place them on warmed serving plates. Drizzle sugar-free chocolate sauce lightly over the pudding and around the plate (optional). Or serve with a fresh fruit sauce.

Serving size: ¹⁄₁₆ of recipe	Calories from fat: 129	Sodium: 138 milligrams
Starch exchanges: 1	Total fat: 14 grams	Carbohydrate: 16 grams
Fat exchanges: 2	Saturated fat: 6 grams	Dietary fiber: 2 grams
Lean-meat exchanges: 1	Cholesterol: 124 milligrams	Sugars: 5 grams
Calories: 209		Protein: 8 grams

Apple Crisp

YIELD: An 8-by-8-inch baking dish

6 Granny Smith apples
Juice of ½ a lemon
½ cup unsweetened apple juice
1 cup plus 2 tablespoons Splenda
  (sugar substitute)
⅓ cup raisins
1 cup low-fat sour cream

3 tablespoons flour
2 eggs
1 teaspoon cinnamon
¼ teaspoon nutmeg
½ cup chopped walnuts
⅓ cup quick oats

Preheat the oven to 350°.

Peel the apples, cut in quarters, and remove cores. Slice into ⅛-inch slices. Place the apples in a heavy saucepan with the lemon juice, apple juice, ½ cup Splenda, and raisins. Place over medium heat and bring the liquid to a boil, stirring constantly. Cover and reduce heat to simmer for 8 to 10 minutes, stirring occasionally. Cook the apples just until soft and remove them from the heat. Transfer to a large mixing bowl and allow to cool.

Place the sour cream in a separate bowl. Sift together the flour and ½ cup Splenda and beat into the sour cream with a wire whisk. Whisk eggs in a small bowl, then beat them into the sour cream mixture. Add ½ teaspoon of the cinnamon and the nutmeg and mix in. Fold the sour cream mixture into the apples and pour into a baking dish coated with cooking spray. Spread out evenly.

In a separate bowl mix together the walnuts, oats, 2 tablespoons Splenda, and the remaining cinnamon. Sprinkle over the top of the apples. Place the baking dish on a cookie sheet in the oven and bake for 25 to 30 minutes, until set. Remove from the oven and cool slightly, for about 20 minutes, before serving.

Serving size: ¹⁄₁₂ of recipe	Calories from fat: 57	Sodium: 22 milligrams
Starch exchanges: 1	Total fat: 6 grams	Carbohydrate: 24 grams
Fruit exchanges: ½	Saturated fat: 2 grams	Dietary fiber: 3 grams
Fat exchanges: 1	Cholesterol: 43 milli-	Sugars: 13 grams
Calories: 161	grams	Protein: 4 grams

Chinese New Year

Celebrated on the first day of the first moon, this holiday usually occurs around the middle of January (the actual date varies from year to year).

Throughout the ages different countries have followed different calendars. For centuries the country of China followed a lunar calendar. It wasn't until early in the twentieth century that China adopted the Gregorian calendar, the one used by almost every other country in the world. The official name of the lunar calendar's New Year is Spring Festival, but its popular name is Chinese New Year.

The New Year is greeted with an all-night celebration centered on the family. Families engage in such activities as board games and cards. Every light in the house is kept on all night long. Fireworks light the sky at midnight, filling the night with noise intended to scare off the evil spirits of the old year. Early the next morning, children receive gifts of money wrapped in red and gold paper.

Families greet relatives, neighbors, and friends in the spirit of reconciliation. The air is permeated with warmth and friendliness, and old grudges are easily shed during this time. The celebration usually goes on for five days, but Chinese New Year is not over until the Festival of Lanterns takes place fifteen days later, at the time of the first full moon of the New Year.

The New Year is said to be the year of a certain animal. Ancient tradition says that the Buddha promised gifts to all the animals that would pay him homage. Twelve animals came to honor Buddha, so each of these animals has a year in the Chinese zodiac named after it. These twelve animals are the Rat, Ox, Tiger, Hare, Dragon, Snake, Horse, Sheep, Monkey, Rooster, Dog, and Boar. The signs repeat every twelve years, and people born in a particular year are said to inherit the characteristics of the animal of the year of their birth.

Individuals born in the Year of the Rat are ambitious and sincere. Those born in the Year of the Ox are bright, cheery, and natural leaders. The Tiger is courageous and sensitive, while the Hare is talented and loving. The Dragon is strong and passionate, and the Snake is wise and strong-willed. Babies born in the Year of the Horse will be attractive and popular, while those born in the Year of the Sheep can claim tasteful and stylish qualities. The Monkey is persuasive and smart, the Rooster is wise and has a pioneering spirit, the Dog is generous and loyal, and the Boar is gallant and noble.

Even if you are not Chinese, you can celebrate this holiday by serving a traditional Chinese meal, complete with chopsticks. It is a great way to teach your children about this culture. Besides conveying an air of authenticity, chopsticks help with portion control. Unless you're very adept at using them, it's hard to overeat!

Chinese New Year

Chicken Daikon Soup

Potstickers

Asian Chicken Salad

Gingered Sea Bass

Chinese Greens and Lo Mein Noodle Stir-Fry

Jasmine Rice Pudding

Note: Many Chinese foods are high in sodium. If you or your guests need to restrict your sodium intake, some of these recipes may not be appropriate.

Chicken Daikon Soup

YIELD: 4 servings

4 cups Chicken Stock (recipe follows)

3 tablespoons rice (long-grain, glutinous)

1 cup daikon (a Chinese radish)*

2 teaspoons ginger, peeled and finely grated

4 ounces chicken breast

¼ cup carrot

1 tablespoon cilantro, chopped

In a 2-quart pot bring the stock to a boil with the rice. Cut the daikon into julienne (long, thin) strips and add to the stock. Add the grated ginger. Turn down the heat and let the broth simmer for 10 minutes. Dice the chicken breast into about ½-inch cubes, cut the carrot into julienne strips,

*If daikon is not available, substitute ½ cup regular radishes.

and add to the simmering broth. Continue to simmer for 15 minutes more. Add the chopped cilantro and turn off the heat. Check for seasoning and add salt or white pepper to taste. Divide into 4 bowls.

Serving size: ¼ recipe	Total fat: 2 grams	Carbohydrate: 10 grams
Vegetable exchanges: 2	Saturated fat: 0 grams	Dietary fiber: 1 gram
Very-lean-meat exchanges: 1	Cholesterol: 12 milligrams	Sugars: 1 gram
Calories: 86	Sodium: 942 milligrams*	Protein: 7 grams
Calories from fat: 17		

Chicken Stock

YIELD: 1½ quarts

3 pounds chicken backs and necks
2 gallons cold water
2 medium onions
2 celery stalks
2 carrots
2 medium tomatoes
1 bunch parsley stems

2 teaspoons thyme
2 teaspoons marjoram
2 bay leaves
2 teaspoons black peppercorns, crushed
2 teaspoons salt (optional)

Rinse the chicken backs and necks. Wash all the vegetables and chop roughly into about ½-inch pieces. Fill a large pot with the water, add the chicken backs and necks, and bring to a boil. Turn the heat down to a slow simmer for 30 minutes. Skim off and discard any impurities that float to the surface. Add all of the vegetables and all of the spices and continue to simmer for 1 hour. Do not let the stock come to a rolling boil, or it may become cloudy. Strain through a fine strainer, cheesecloth, or coffee filter to remove all particles. Discard the bones and the vegetables.

*This recipe is not recommended for low-sodium diets.

This stock should be clear, with a slight golden hue. Adjust the seasoning if desired.

Note: Freeze any remaining stock in small containers for use in other recipes.

Serving size: 5⅓ ounces	Saturated fat: 0 grams	Dietary fiber: 0 grams
Free food	Cholesterol: 0 milligrams	Sugars: 0 grams
Calories: 20	Sodium: 516 (129)*	Protein: 1 gram
Calories from fat: 12	milligrams	
Total fat: 1 gram	Carbohydrate: 1 gram	

Potstickers

YIELD: Approximately 20 dumplings (10 servings)

¼ cup finely chopped green cabbage
4 ounces lean pork, chopped into very small pieces or coarsely ground
1 tablespoon low-sodium soy sauce
1 teaspoon sugar
1 teaspoon sesame oil
1 teaspoon oyster sauce†
1 whole green onion, chopped
1 teaspoon peeled and finely grated fresh ginger

⅔ cup Potsticker Dipping Sauce (recipe follows)
20 round gyoza (wonton) wrappers or skins† (leftover wrappers can be frozen if wrapped tightly and used later)
Scant tablespoon canola oil

Blanch the cabbage for 1 minute in boiling water and drain in a strainer. While the cabbage is draining, put the pork in a bowl with the other ingredients (except for the dipping sauce and wrappers) and mix well. Squeeze the cabbage dry and add to the pork mixture. Place a scant tablespoon of the mixture in the center of a wrapper. Wet the edges of the

*Figure in parentheses does not include salt.
†Available wherever Chinese foods are sold.

wrapper with water and fold in half. Starting at one end, pinch the curved edge together, making 4 or 5 pleats. Cover with a damp cloth while making the remaining potstickers.

Heat a wide nonstick fry pan on medium-high heat and add a scant tablespoon of oil. Put the potstickers in pleated edge up, not touching one another. Cook for about 2 to 3 minutes or until the bottoms are golden brown. Drain the excess oil, turn the heat down to medium low, and add ⅓ cup of water. Cover and steam for about 5 minutes or until all the liquid has evaporated. If you have more potstickers to cook and steam, keep the steamed ones warm in a 200° oven while repeating the process. Serve 2 potstickers with about 1 tablespoon of dipping sauce as an appetizer.

Note: Potstickers can be made in advance. After pleating the potstickers, place them in the freezer flat on a tray, not touching. When frozen, they can be transferred to airtight bags. The day before you are ready to cook, take them out of the freezer and place them flat on a tray. Cover and defrost in the refrigerator overnight. Cook as described above.

Serving size: 2 pot- stickers	Calories from fat: 51	Carbohydrate: 11 grams
	Total fat: 6 grams	Dietary fiber: 0 grams
Starch exchanges: 1	Saturated fat: 1 gram	Sugars: 1 gram
Fat exchanges: 1	Cholesterol: 9 milligrams	Protein: 5 grams
Calories: 123	Sodium: 615 milligrams*	

Potsticker Dipping Sauce

YIELD: Approximately 2 cups

1 cup low-sodium soy sauce
½ cup water
⅓ cup rice wine vinegar
2 packages Sweet'N Low

1 teaspoon peeled and finely minced
    fresh ginger
1 green onion, finely sliced

*This recipe is not recommended for low-sodium diets.

Bring all the ingredients to a boil, except for the green onion. Turn off the heat and allow the mixture to cool down. Add the slices of green onion. Serve cold with potstickers.

Serving size: 1 table- spoon Free food Calories: 8 Calories from fat: 0	Total fat: 0 grams Saturated fat: 0 grams Cholesterol: 0 milligrams Sodium: 400 milligrams* Carbohydrate: 1 gram	Dietary fiber: 0 grams Sugars: 0 grams Protein: 1 gram

Asian Chicken Salad

YIELD: 6 servings

Chicken

2 tablespoons low-sodium soy sauce
1 packet Sweet'N Low
2 tablespoons water

8 ounces skinless and boneless
    chicken breasts

In a small bowl, mix the soy sauce, Sweet'N Low, and water. Pour this over the chicken, cover tightly, refrigerate, and marinate for 24 hours. Remove the chicken from the marinade and broil until the internal temperature reaches 165° in the thickest part, or approximately 5 to 6 minutes per side. Let cool. Cut each breast in half, and then cut into thin slices to make strips ¼ inch thick and 2 inches long.

*This recipe is not recommended for low-sodium diets.

Dressing

YIELD: 3 ounces

4 teaspoons Hoisin sauce*
¼ teaspoon ground ginger
1 teaspoon Dijon mustard
4 teaspoons chili sauce

1 teaspoon peanut butter
4 teaspoons rice vinegar
1 teaspoon sesame oil
5 teaspoons canola oil

In a bowl, blend all the ingredients except for the oils. Add the oils slowly while whisking to fully incorporate them.

Salad

1 teaspoon chopped cilantro
1 tablespoon thinly sliced green onions
1 tablespoon grated carrot
1 cup chopped romaine lettuce
1 cup chopped iceberg lettuce

½ cup thinly sliced red cabbage
1 cup napa cabbage, sliced in thin strips
8 ounces cooked chicken breast, already prepared
Dressing (3 ounces), already prepared

To prepare the salad for serving, mix the salad ingredients with the chicken and toss well with the dressing. Serve in 6 chilled bowls or 1 large bowl if you are having a buffet-style meal.

Serving size: ⅙ of recipe	Calories from fat: 52	Carbohydrate: 4 grams
Very-lean-meat exchanges: 1	Total fat: 6 grams	Dietary fiber: 1 gram
Vegetable exchanges: 1	Saturated fat: 1 gram	Sugars: 1 gram
Fat exchanges: 1	Cholesterol: 24 milli-grams	Protein: 9 grams
Calories: 107	Sodium: 170 milligrams	

*Available wherever Chinese foods are sold.

Gingered Sea Bass

YIELD: 4 servings

1 whole sea bass, about 1½–2 pounds, cleaned and scaled
½ small red pepper, sliced into thin strips
4 tablespoons thinly sliced green onions

2 tablespoons peeled and grated ginger
1 small jalapeño pepper, thinly sliced
1 tablespoon chopped cilantro
1 tablespoon soy sauce
1 teaspoon sesame oil (optional)

Wash the fish under cold water and pat it dry with paper towels. With a sharp knife, make 4 or 5 deep diagonal cuts about 1 inch apart down to the bone on both sides. Lay the fish on a heatproof platter about ½ inch smaller than your steamer. (If you do not have a steamer, use a pan with a rack.) Top the fish with all the vegetables, reserving half of the green onion. Place the platter in the steamer and steam, covered, over boiling water for about 12 to 15 minutes, or until the fish is opaque or flaky at the thickest part. Transfer the fish to a serving platter. Sprinkle it with the soy sauce, 1 teaspoon sesame oil (optional), and the reserved green onion.

Serving size: ¼ recipe	Total fat: 3 grams	Carbohydrate: 3 grams
Very-lean-meat exchanges: 4	Saturated fat: 1 gram	Dietary fiber: 1 gram
	Cholesterol: 61 milli-	Sugars: 1 gram
Calories: 158	grams	Protein: 28 grams
Calories from fat: 27	Sodium: 350 milligrams*	

*This recipe is not recommended for low-sodium diets.

Chinese Greens and Lo Mein Noodle Stir-Fry

YIELD: 8 servings

8 ounces lo mein noodles*
1 clove garlic, minced
1 medium onion, sliced
2 medium carrots, thinly sliced, bias cut
2 stalks celery, thinly sliced, bias cut
¼ cup daikon (or ⅛ cup radish), julienne cut (long, thin strips)
1 tablespoon canola oil

1 medium Portabella mushroom (discard stem), thinly sliced
½ head napa cabbage, shredded
2 tablespoons low-sodium soy sauce
1 cup bean sprouts
2 tablespoons cornstarch mixed with 2 tablespoons cold water
2 green onions, chopped

Cook the noodles according to the package directions, then rinse them under cold running water and drain.

Blanch the garlic, onion, carrots, celery, and daikon in 2 inches of boiling water until about ¾ cooked, or for about 2 minutes after the water returns to a boil.

Heat the oil over high heat in a large wok or frying pan. Add the blanched vegetables with the Portabella mushroom and stir for 1 minute. Turn heat to medium-high, add the cabbage, and continue to cook, covered, for 3 minutes. Add the soy sauce and bean sprouts and cook, covered, for 1 minute over high heat. Move vegetables to the outer edge of the wok or pan. Thicken the liquid with the cornstarch/water mixture and stir. Add the drained noodles to the vegetables. Stir well over high heat for 1 minute. Divide onto 4 plates and top with green onion.

The noodles can be cooked in advance.

Serving size: ⅛ recipe	Total fat: 2 grams	Carbohydrate: 32 grams
Starch exchanges: 2	Saturated fat: 0 grams	Dietary fiber: 2 grams
Calories: 149	Cholesterol: 0 milligrams	Sugars: 3 grams
Calories from fat: 17	Sodium: 173 milligrams	Protein: 2 grams

*Available wherever Chinese foods are sold.

Jasmine Rice Pudding

YIELD: 6 servings

3 cups water
½ cup jasmine rice*
1 cup 2% milk
½ cup Splenda (sugar substitute)

½ teaspoon vanilla extract
⅓ cup golden raisins
¼ teaspoon cinnamon
6 mint leaves

Pour the water into a large saucepan and bring it to a boil. Add the rice, return to a boil, and then reduce the heat to simmer. Cook the rice approximately 12 to 15 minutes, until it is soft. The liquid will be reduced by half. Add the milk, Splenda, and vanilla. Simmer, stirring occasionally, for about 20 minutes, until the mixture is creamy. Stir in the raisins and cinnamon, then turn off the heat and let cool. Pour into serving dishes and chill. Immediately before serving, garnish each portion with a mint leaf.

Serving size: ½ cup	Total fat: 1 gram	Carbohydrate: 24 grams
Starch exchanges: 1½	Saturated fat: 0 grams	Dietary fiber: 1 gram
Calories: 114	Cholesterol: 3 milligrams	Sugars: 8 grams
Calories from fat: 7	Sodium: 28 milligrams	Protein: 3 grams

*Jasmine rice is a long-grain aromatic rice with a subtle perfume. It is ideal for rice pudding, as it is moist and tender, not fluffy, when cooked.

February

Valentine's Day

Valentine's Day

February 14

V alentine's Day is an international holiday celebrated in France, England, Canada, and the United States. Legend tells us that it is named for the patron saint of lovers—a Roman priest, St. Valentine, whom the Romans martyred on February 14, 271, because he would not renounce his Christian faith. Two versions of the origin of this holiday exist according to folklore accounts. One is that St. Valentine wrote messages of love, hope, and cheer to his family and friends while imprisoned, sending these messages via carrier pigeon. Another version is that he wrote a note just before he was executed to the daughter of the jailer who had befriended him—and signed it "Your Valentine."

Over the years lots of traditions have blossomed in observance of Valentine's Day. Greeting cards originated in England toward the end of the nineteenth century, featuring a heart or a cupid; they were decorated with satin, lace, and ribbons. Birds now are often featured on valentine cards, because they mate for life and thus are a symbol of true lifelong love. Plus, legend has it that birds have always been messengers and that they delivered the very first valentines. Frequently greeting cards were sent anonymously and signed simply "Your Valentine."

While candy, especially chocolate candy, is a common gift for Valentine's Day in the twenty-first century, it is not a part of the origins of this holiday. So if you wish, you can be very authentic and plan your celebration without it.

If you are planning a party for children and one of those children happens to have diabetes, you may wish to focus on some craft activities. Gather supplies like red construction paper or leftover red Christmas wrapping paper and ribbon, lace, glitter, and glue, and let the children make a valentine card for a special person in their life. Read, or ask another adult to read, the children a story on the history of Valentine's Day as one of the party activities. They will learn the true meaning of the day (and you will have a few minutes of quiet in the midst of chaos!).

If the party is for yourself and an admirer, go all out on decor! Set the table with your most elegant linens, china, and crystal. If you do not have elegant tableware, choose pretty and affordable disposables from your local card or party shop. Buy an inexpensive piece of red fabric or plastic to cover your table, and then cover it with a white or ivory-colored lace tablecloth. This attractive tablecloth can be used not only for Valentine's Day but for any celebration with red in the color scheme!

Note: Don't forget fresh flowers and candles, which can make even the most mundane meal elegant!

Valentine's Day

Potato and Caviar Hors d'Oeuvres

Valentine Salad with Raspberry Vinaigrette

Veal Scalloppini Marsala

Wild Rice

Broccoli Parmesan

Strawberry-Chocolate Cream Delight

or

Sorbet with Berry Coulis

Potato and Caviar Hors d'Oeuvres

YIELD: 2 servings

4 very small egg-shaped white or red skin potatoes

2 teaspoons sour cream

½ teaspoon finely chopped onion or finely chopped chives

½ ounce sevruga caviar

In a small pot, with about 2 cups of water, simmer the potatoes gently for 30 minutes. Place them in the refrigerator to cool in the water they were cooked in. (This step can be done the day before.) When potatoes are cold, after about an hour, cut a small piece off one end of each, so the potato will stand up. Cut off the top third of the potato at a 45-degree angle and discard. Using a teaspoon, scoop out a small cavity about ¾ inch deep from the center of the potato. Into each cavity place ½ teaspoon of sour cream and ⅛ teaspoon of the onions or chives, and top with a fourth of the caviar. Do this for each potato. Refrigerate until ready to serve.

Serving size: ½ recipe	Saturated fat: 1 gram	Dietary fiber: 1 gram
Starch exchanges: 1	Cholesterol: 43 milli-	Sugars: 1 gram
Calories: 85	grams	Protein: 3 grams
Calories from fat: 19	Sodium: 112 milligrams	
Total fat: 2 grams	Carbohydrate: 14 grams	

Valentine Salad with Raspberry Vinaigrette

YIELD: 2 servings

4 slices sourdough bread
1 rounded teaspoon very soft butter
  or margarine (optional)
2 cups assorted baby field greens

1 recipe Raspberry Vinaigrette
  (recipe follows)
8 fresh raspberries, if available, or
  defrosted frozen raspberries

Cut out 4 heart-shaped croutons from the bread (utilize the remaining bread for crumbs or another use). Very lightly butter each crouton (butter, or margarine, is optional) and toast in a hot oven until lightly brown.

Toss the greens with the Raspberry Vinaigrette and place them on chilled salad plates. Place the raspberries evenly around the plates. Top with the heart-shaped croutons.

Serving size: ½ recipe	Total fat: 4 grams	Dietary fiber: 2 grams
Starch exchanges: 1	Saturated fat: 2 grams	Sugars: 3 grams
Fat exchanges: 1	Cholesterol: 7 milligrams	Protein: 4 grams
Calories: 127	Sodium: 194 milligrams	
Calories from fat: 36	Carbohydrate: 18 grams	

Salad with unbuttered croutons

Serving size: ½ recipe	Total fat: 1 gram	Carbohydrate: 18 grams
Starch exchanges: 1	Saturated fat: 0 grams	Dietary fiber: 2 grams
Calories: 100	Cholesterol: 1 milligram	Sugars: 3 grams
Calories from fat: 8	Sodium: 174 milligrams	Protein: 4 grams

Salad with no croutons

Serving size: ½ recipe	Total fat: 0 grams	Carbohydrate: 5 grams
Vegetable exchanges: 1	Saturated fat: 0 grams	Dietary fiber: 2 grams
Calories: 32	Cholesterol: 1 milligram	Sugars: 3 grams
Calories from fat: 2	Sodium: 22 milligrams	Protein: 2 grams

Raspberry Vinaigrette

YIELD: 2 servings

2 tablespoons plain nonfat yogurt
2 teaspoons white wine vinegar or
   champagne vinegar

½ teaspoon Splenda (sugar substitute)
¼ cup defrosted raspberries (or
   fresh, if available)

In a small dish, blend all ingredients well, mashing the raspberries. Push through a fine sieve to remove all the seeds. Cover and refrigerate until ready to serve. This is best if made the day before.

Serving size: ½ recipe	Total fat: 0 grams	Carbohydrate: 3 grams
Free food	Saturated fat: 0 grams	Dietary fiber: 0 grams
Calories: 19	Cholesterol: 1 milligram	Sugars: 2 grams
Calories from fat: 0	Sodium: 12 milligrams	Protein: 1 gram

Veal Scalloppini Marsala

YIELD: 2 servings

4 3-ounce slices of veal,* pounded
  to ¹⁄₁₆ inch thick (ask the butcher
  to cut the veal slices from the leg
  or, if possible, the loin, and ask to
  have them flattened to ¹⁄₁₆ inch
  thick)

1 tablespoon olive oil
1 tablespoon finely diced onion
6 ounces mushrooms, washed, and
  sliced
½ cup marsala wine (or water)
1 teaspoon chopped fresh parsley

Dust the veal lightly with flour. Heat a 10- or 12-inch sauté pan on high, add the olive oil, and quickly sauté the veal slices about 1 minute on each side, or until lightly browned. Transfer to a warm platter. Turn the heat down to medium. Add the onion and mushrooms and sauté for 5 minutes. Add the marsala wine and bring to a boil, stirring the bottom of the pan to loosen any browned particles. Once the wine comes to a boil, 85 to 90 percent of the alcohol will be burned off, leaving only the flavor. After 1 minute of boiling, return the veal to the pan, along with any juices from the platter. Turn off the heat. Take the veal out of pan and place it on plates. Add the parsley to the pan, stir, and spoon the mushroom marsala sauce over the veal.

Serving size: ½ recipe	Total fat: 11 grams	Dietary fiber: 1 gram
Very-lean-meat exchanges: 5	Saturated fat: 2 grams	Sugars: 2 grams
Fat exchanges: 2	Cholesterol: 132 milligrams	Protein: 39 grams
Calories: 274†	Sodium: 92 milligrams	Alcohol: 1 gram†
Calories from fat: 100	Carbohydrate: 3 grams	

*If you prefer, this recipe easily adapts to chicken. Use skinless, boneless breasts flattened thin instead of the veal. The chicken will take just a little longer to cook (about 2 to 3 minutes longer each side).
†If you substitute water for marsala wine, you will save 1 gram of alcohol and 7 calories per serving. However, the flavor will not be as rich.

Wild Rice

YIELD: 2 servings

1 teaspoon olive oil
1 tablespoon minced onion
1 clove garlic, minced
½ small red bell pepper, chopped
  fine
¼ cup wild rice

1 cup Chicken Stock (see recipe,
  p. 21)
⅛ cup pecans, chopped small
1 tablespoon finely chopped fresh
  parsley

In a 1-quart pot on medium heat, add the olive oil, onion, garlic, red bell pepper, and rice. Sauté for 2 minutes. Add the chicken stock and the pecans. Cover, bring to a boil, and then turn down the heat to a slow simmer for 50 minutes. Add chopped parsley and serve.

Serving size: ½ recipe, about ½ cup	Calories from fat: 75	Carbohydrate: 20 grams
Starch exchanges: 1	Total fat: 8 grams	Dietary fiber: 3 grams
Fat exchanges: 1½	Saturated fat: 1 gram	Sugars: 1 gram
Calories: 165	Cholesterol: 1 milligram	Protein: 5 grams
	Sodium: 371 milligrams*	

Broccoli Parmesan

YIELD: 2 servings

8 ounces fresh broccoli   1 tablespoon Parmesan cheese

Cut the head of the broccoli off the stem just at the point where the head will stay in one piece. Cut the stem to a 3-inch length and discard the thick portion of the remaining stem. Cut the remaining stem into 4 pieces

*This recipe is not recommended for low-sodium diets. You can substitute low-sodium chicken stock to reduce the sodium.

lengthwise. Cut the head in half. Add water to a level in a pot just below bottom of a steamer basket and bring to a boil. Add the broccoli stems and cook for 4 minutes, covered. Add the broccoli heads. Cover and continue to steam for another 4 minutes or until tender. Sprinkle with the Parmesan cheese just prior to serving.

Serving size: 4 ounces	Total fat: 1 gram	Carbohydrate: 6 grams
Vegetable exchanges: 1	Saturated fat: 1 gram	Dietary fiber: 3 grams
Calories: 43	Cholesterol: 2 milligrams	Sugars: 2 grams
Calories from fat: 10	Sodium: 77 milligrams	Protein: 4 grams

Strawberry-Chocolate Cream Delight

YIELD: 2 servings

½ cup Cool Whip Lite whipped topping
¾ teaspoon cocoa powder

6 strawberries (with stems, if possible)
1 small banana

Whisk together the topping with the cocoa powder until completely combined. (If the cocoa powder is lumpy, sift it first.) Wash the strawberries and dry, leaving the stems on if you like. Peel the banana and slice it in half lengthwise, and then cut each half in 3 pieces. To serve, place the chocolate cream in the center of a dessert plate and arrange the fruit around it.

Note: You can also serve the dessert with pineapple spears, melon cubes, or even fresh orange segments. Use any fruit that could be picked up as finger food and dipped in cream to eat.

Serving size: ½ recipe	Total fat: 3 grams	Dietary fiber: 2 grams
Fruit exchanges: 1	Saturated fat: 2 grams	Sugars: 13 grams
Fat exchanges: 1	Cholesterol: 0 milligrams	Protein: 1 gram
Calories: 113	Sodium: 3 milligrams	
Calories from fat: 25	Carbohydrate: 21 grams	

Sorbet with Berry Coulis

YIELD: 2 servings

½ cup individually quick frozen
  raspberries
2 tablespoons fresh orange juice
½ teaspoon Equal (1½ packets)

1 cup fresh or individually quick
  frozen mixed berries
1 cup fruit sorbet, any flavor

If you are using frozen berries, first lay them out in a single layer on a plate to thaw.

Put the raspberries and orange juice in a heavy saucepan over low heat. Cook slowly, stirring occasionally, approximately 5 minutes, or until the raspberries fall apart. Squeeze through a fine strainer to extract all the juice. Discard the seeds. Stir the Equal into the juice. Fold in the mixed berries. Serve over the fruit sorbet.

Serving size: ½ recipe	Total fat: 0 grams	Carbohydrate: 41 grams
Fruit exchanges: 3	Saturated fat: 0 grams	Dietary fiber: 3 grams
Calories: 172	Cholesterol: 0 milligrams	Sugars: 34 grams
Calories from fat: 0	Sodium: 5 milligrams	Protein: 1 gram

March

St. Patrick's Day

St. Patrick's Day

March 17

St. Patrick's Day is held in celebration of a man who lived and died sixteen centuries ago. St. Patrick was born in England in about A.D. 389. When he was sixteen years old, he was abducted by pirates and sold into slavery in Ireland. He escaped six years later and went to study at a European monastery. He became a priest and then a bishop, after which he returned to Ireland, where he brought Christianity and literacy to the people. He started many churches and schools whose traditions live on to this very day. Now he is known as the patron saint of literacy.

A great teacher, St. Patrick used common, everyday things to explain complex concepts. He used the shamrock, today a symbol of Irish heritage, to represent the trinity of God the Father, the Son, and the Holy Spirit. The shamrock is a type of clover that grows abundantly in Ireland and contributes to the beautiful green color of the landscape. Thus Ireland holds the nickname "The Emerald Isle."

In Ireland, St. Patrick's Day traditionally is a solemn celebration, honoring the anniversary of the death of this great saint. In the United States and other countries where Irish immigrants have settled, it takes on a more festive tone. Parades, the wearin' of the green, and parties are the order of the day.

Many people immigrated to the United States when the potato famine hit Ireland, and legend now has it that there are more people of Irish descent in this country than there are in Ireland. This is not all that surprising, however, when you think about the fact that over half the people who fought in the Revolutionary War had Irish ancestors. In this century it seems that everyone with a drop of Irish blood celebrates on March 17. So if you are planning a party and including guests who have diabetes or other health concerns, do not omit traditional Irish favorites. This Split Pea Soup is an appropriate starter, because of its color. But it is a hearty soup and, for some, may just make the whole meal. Corned beef, cabbage, and boiled potatoes are found on restaurant menus for this holiday everywhere, but the recipes here will help you make lower-fat versions of these favorites. Irish Soda Bread is another traditional food you may want to try.

St. Patrick's Day

Split Pea Soup

New World Corned Beef and Cabbage

Irish Soda Bread

Mint Parfaits

Split Pea Soup

YIELD: 8 servings

1 ham hock, smoked (about 8 ounces)
1 16-ounce package dried split peas
2 medium (1 cup) carrots, diced small
1 medium (1 cup) onion, diced small
1 clove garlic, finely minced
1 bay leaf
¼ teaspoon white pepper
1 cup peeled and grated potatoes
8 cups water

Place all ingredients in a 4-quart pot or Dutch oven and bring to a boil over high heat. Reduce heat to low, cover, and simmer slowly for 2 hours. Remove the ham hock, discarding skin, bone, and gristle. Cut the meat into small cubes and add back into the soup. If you like the soup to be smooth, carefully pour it into a blender (to only half full) and puree for a few seconds. Repeat until all the soup has been pureed. Put the soup back on the stove and heat while stirring until it comes back to a boil. Serves 12 (5⅓-ounce portions) as a starter or 6 as a meal on a cold winter night.

Serving size: 5⅓ ounces	Total fat: 1 gram	Carbohydrate: 28 grams
Starch exchanges: 2	Saturated fat: 0 grams	Dietary fiber: 10 grams
Calories: 160	Cholesterol: 2 milligrams	Sugars: 4 grams
Calories from fat: 10	Sodium: 73 milligrams	Protein: 11 grams

New World Corned Beef and Cabbage

YIELD: 6 servings

1 corned beef brisket, first cut or flat
   cut
1 medium onion, cut in half, then
   sliced ¼ inch thick
2 cloves garlic, cut in half and
   smashed

6 small red-skinned potatoes, washed
1 small head savoy cabbage
2 medium carrots, sliced ¼ inch
   thick

Fill a very large pot halfway with water. Bring the water to a boil. Rinse the corned beef in cold water so that all pickling spice is removed and add it to the pot. Add the onion and garlic and cover. Turn the heat down and simmer for 1¾ hours. Add the potatoes and continue to cook for 30 minutes. Cut the cabbage into wedges, leaving the core intact, and add them to the pot with the carrots. Cover and simmer an additional 15 minutes. Carefully lift out the cabbage wedges with a perforated spoon or scoop and let them drain. Pull out the meat and let it rest for 5 minutes on a cutting board. Portion out the potatoes, onions, carrots, and cabbage. Slice the corned beef against the grain in thin slices and serve with the vegetables.

Note: You will have corned beef left over for another meal. Leftover corned beef can be stored, covered, in its cooking water in the refrigerator.

Serving size: 3 ounces of corned beef, ⅙ of the vegetables	Calories: 293	Sodium: 1045 milligrams*
	Calories from fat: 84	
	Total fat: 9 grams	Carbohydrate: 31 grams
Starch exchanges: 1	Saturated fat: 3 grams	Dietary fiber: 8 grams
Vegetable exchanges: 2	Cholesterol: 83 milligrams	Sugars: 7 grams
Lean-meat exchanges: 3		Protein: 22 grams

*This recipe is not recommended for low-sodium diets.

Irish Soda Bread

YIELD: 16 servings

2 cups all-purpose flour
1 teaspoon baking soda
½ teaspoon salt
2 tablespoons butter, chopped

2 teaspoons caraway seeds
½ cup golden raisins
6½ ounces buttermilk

Preheat the oven to 375°.

Sift together the flour, baking soda, and salt. Place in the bowl of a mixer fitted with the paddle attachment. Add the chopped butter; cut it in until the mixture resembles coarse cornmeal. Add the caraway seeds, raisins, and buttermilk. Mix only to combine. Turn out the dough onto a lightly floured surface. Knead it just enough to shape into a circle and press evenly into a greased 9-inch round cake pan. Cut a cross on top about 1 inch deep. Bake for approximately 25 minutes, until the top of the bread is lightly browned. The loaf will sound hollow when tapped.

Serving size: ¹⁄₁₆ of loaf	Total fat: 2 grams	Carbohydrate: 17 grams
Starch exchanges: 1	Saturated fat: 1 gram	Dietary fiber: 1 gram
Calories: 92	Cholesterol: 5 milligrams	Sugars: 4 grams
Calories from fat: 16	Sodium: 169 milligrams	Protein: 2 grams

Mint Parfait

YIELD: 6 servings

½ cup egg substitute
4 teaspoons Equal (13 packets)
3 tablespoons green crème de
  menthe (optional)
¼ teaspoon mint extract
2½ cups Cool Whip Lite whipped
  topping

1½ tablespoons crushed Oreo cookie
  crumbs (cookie part only, no
  filling)
6 mint leaves for garnish (if available)

Place the egg substitute and Equal into the bowl of an electric mixer fitted with the whip attachment and whip up until light and fluffy. Add crème de menthe and mint extract, and mix in. By hand, fold in 2 cups of the whipped topping along with the Oreo crumbs. Spoon mixture into parfait glasses or other appropriate glasses that can go into the freezer; freeze for at least 6 hours before serving. To serve, top each glass with a dollop of the remaining whipped topping and a mint leaf.

Serving size: 1 parfait	Total fat: 4 grams	Dietary fiber: 0 grams
Starch exchanges: 1	Saturated fat: 4 grams	Sugars: 7 grams
Fat exchanges: 1	Cholesterol: 0 milligrams	Protein: 3 grams
Calories: 134*	Sodium: 55 milligrams	Alcohol: 3 grams*
Calories from fat: 40	Carbohydrate: 14 grams	

*If you choose to leave the crème de menthe out of this recipe, you will save 3 grams of alcohol and 21 calories. You could use green food coloring to color your parfait, but unfortunately there is no nonalcoholic substitute for flavor.

April

Easter
Passover

Easter

First Sunday after the first full moon of the spring equinox

*E*aster is the most important holiday in the Christian religion. This joyous, solemn Christian observance celebrates the resurrection of Jesus. The New Testament says that Jesus rose from the dead on the third day after he had been crucified, disappearing from the tomb where he was buried. This miracle fulfilled God's promise to send his son to redeem mortal men and save them for all eternity. Easter climaxes the forty days of Lent, a time of fasting and prayer, that began on Ash Wednesday. Easter Sunday is celebrated in Christian countries around the world. It is a day of rejoicing, when Christian churches are decorated with spring flowers, Easter lilies abound, and joyous music fills the air.

The word "Easter" can be traced back to the Anglo-Saxon name for the goddess of spring and fertility, Eostra. Back then people celebrated with a spring festival named after the goddess, which welcomed the rebirth of nature long before the era of Christianity. The hare was the symbol for Eostra and is thus a forerunner of the modern-day Easter Bunny and the basket of eggs he brings. Today Easter eggs symbolize Christ's resurrection from the dead and the rebirth of new life in spring. Colored and decorated eggs have long been a part of the Easter tradition. They originated in Egypt and Persia; the custom was probably brought to Europe by travelers, immigrants, and traders.

Another long-standing Easter custom is dressing in new clothes, and for years a new hat worn at this time was affectionately referred to as an "Easter bonnet." In 1933, Irving Berlin immortalized the custom with his classic hit "Easter Parade" which we still hear today. Old-movie buffs might want to rent the movie of the same name, starring Fred Astaire and Judy Garland.

Wherever you are, you may want to make a very special dinner for this holiday. Roast Spring Leg of Lamb is an appropriate and tasty entrée, accompanied by Garlic Red Potatoes and Fresh Asparagus Polonaise. Start with a Spring Garden Vegetable Salad dressed with Lemon Vinaigrette. Top off your feast with a small piece of Easter Orange Cheesecake or Strawberry Chiffon Parfait. For a special treat you may want to make homemade Pumpernickel Dinner Rolls. You can mix the dough in your bread machine or, if you prefer, by hand. Your family and guests will know they are special when you all sit down to this delectable meal.

If your child has diabetes, do something extraordinary for him or her. Concentrate on getting a new Easter outfit or decorating Easter eggs. You might even consider hosting an egg-decorating party with a few friends on the day before Easter. Let your child help make an Easter centerpiece filled with fresh spring flowers and the eggs you've decorated.

Easter

Spring Garden Vegetable Salad with Lemon Vinaigrette

Roast Spring Leg of Lamb with Mint Sauce

Garlic Red Potatoes

Asparagus Polonaise

Pumpernickel Dinner Rolls

Easter Orange Cheesecake

or

Strawberry Chiffon Parfait

Spring Garden Vegetable Salad

YIELD: 4 servings

4 slices turkey bacon
½ pound dandelion greens, washed and dried
2 tablespoons finely diced red onion
4 ounces mushrooms, washed and thinly sliced

1 hard-boiled egg, cooled and chopped small
Lemon Vinaigrette (recipe follows)

Cut the strips of bacon in half lengthwise, then every ½ inch across. Cook the bacon in a fry pan until it is brown and crispy. Drain and set on paper towels to absorb any grease. Toss all ingredients in a large bowl. Serve with Lemon Vinaigrette.

Serving size: ¼ recipe	Total fat: 5 grams	Carbohydrate: 6 grams
Vegetable exchanges: 1	Saturated fat: 1 gram	Dietary fiber: 2 grams
Fat exchanges: 1	Cholesterol: 63 milli-	Sugars: 2 grams
Calories: 84	grams	Protein: 6 grams
Calories from fat: 42	Sodium: 250 milligrams	

Lemon Vinaigrette

YIELD: 4 servings

2 teaspoons Dijon mustard
1 tablespoon fresh lemon juice
1½ tablespoons rice wine vinegar
3 tablespoons virgin olive oil

Pinch of salt
Pinch of pepper
1 tablespoon peeled, seeded, and
   finely diced lemon

Place the Dijon mustard, lemon juice, and vinegar in a bowl or blender. Slowly add the oil while whisking constantly. Season with salt and pepper to taste. Add lemon to the dressing.

Serving size: 2 table-	Total fat: 11 grams	Dietary fiber: 0 grams
spoons	Saturated fat: 2 grams	Sugars: 0 grams
Fat exchanges: 2	Cholesterol: 0 milligrams	Protein: 0 grams
Calories: 97	Sodium: 51 milligrams	
Calories from fat: 96	Carbohydrate: 1 gram	

Roast Spring Leg of Lamb

YIELD: 6 servings

1 6-pound leg of lamb, shank half,
  pelvic bone removed
2 teaspoons olive oil
1 tablespoon Dijon mustard

1 tablespoon fresh lemon juice
2 cloves garlic, very finely minced
2 teaspoons fresh rosemary chopped
  small

Remove all excess fat from the lamb as well as the pelvic bone, if still attached.

In a bowl, combine the olive oil, mustard, lemon juice, minced garlic, and rosemary. Rub this mixture all over the leg of lamb and marinate in the refrigerator for at least 1 hour.

Preheat the oven to 400°.

Season the lamb with salt and pepper and roast for 15 minutes. Reduce the temperature to 325° and continue to roast for approximately 1½ hours, or until the internal temperature reading of a meat thermometer inserted into the center of the thickest part reaches 135°. Let the lamb rest out of the oven for 20 minutes before slicing. The inside should still be slightly pink and juicy.

Serving size: 3 ounces	Total fat: 12 grams	Carbohydrate: 0 grams
Medium-fat-meat	Saturated fat: 5 grams	Dietary fiber: 0 grams
exchanges: 3	Cholesterol: 77 milli-	Sugars: 0 grams
Calories: 210	grams	Protein: 23 grams
Calories from fat: 110	Sodium: 65 milligrams	

Mint Sauce

YIELD: 6 servings

1 tablespoon onion, finely chopped
1 teaspoon olive oil
1¼ cups chopped and loosely
　packed fresh mint leaves

¼ cup dry white wine (or water)
¼ cup water
4 tablespoons vinegar
4 teaspoons Splenda (sugar substitute)

In a small saucepan over medium-high heat, sauté the onion in the olive oil for 2 to 3 minutes, stirring often, until translucent. Add 1 cup of the chopped mint leaves, stir well, and continue to cook for 1 minute. Add the wine, water, vinegar, and Splenda. Turn the heat down and simmer for 10 minutes. Strain. Let cool for 15 minutes and add remaining mint leaves. Cover and refrigerate until ready to serve.

Serving size: 1 table-　spoon	Total fat: 1 gram	Dietary fiber: 0 grams
Free food	Saturated fat: 0 grams	Sugars: 0 grams
Calories: 15*	Cholesterol: 0 milligrams	Protein: 0 grams
Calories from fat: 6	Sodium: 1 milligram	Alcohol: ½ gram*
	Carbohydrate: 1 gram	

Garlic Red Potatoes

YIELD: 6 servings

6 red potatoes, golf ball size
1½ cups water

1 teaspoon salt
1 teaspoon dried minced garlic

Select potatoes that are all about the same size. If you purchase the very small (in diameter) potatoes, figure 2 per person and shorten the cooking time by about 5 minutes.

*If you substitute water for wine, you will save ½ gram of alcohol and 3 calories.

Wash the potatoes well. With a potato peeler or sharp knife, peel about a ½-inch-wide band around the center of the potato. Place all the ingredients into a pot. Bring to a boil, then turn the heat down to simmer, cover, and cook for 25 to 30 minutes depending on potato size. Check that the water is simmering and not at a fast boil. A fast boil will tear the skins.

Test for doneness by inserting a fork into the center of a potato. If it comes out easily, the potatoes are done.

Serving size: 1 potato	Total fat: 0 grams	Carbohydrate: 17 grams
Starch exchanges: 1	Saturated fat: 0 grams	Dietary fiber: 0 grams
Calories: 79	Cholesterol: 0 milligrams	Sugars: 0 grams
Calories from fat: 1	Sodium: 119 milligrams	Protein: 3 grams

Asparagus Polonaise

YIELD: 6 servings

2 pounds green asparagus, jumbo or medium size*
4 slices white bread, crusts removed
1 cup Chicken Stock (see recipe, p. 21)
2 teaspoons olive oil
White of 1 hard-boiled egg, finely chopped

1 tablespoon finely chopped fresh parsley
⅛ teaspoon white pepper
⅛ teaspoon light chili powder
⅛ teaspoon onion powder

Hold each end of an asparagus stalk and bend until it snaps. Discard the short stem. You are now left with a tender stalk. Repeat this process with the remaining stalks. With a vegetable peeler, peel about 2 to 3 inches of the base end of each asparagus spear. This will give the stem of the asparagus a light green color; the tips will be dark green.

Bring 2 inches of water to a boil in a 4-quart pot. Place a steamer basket in the pot. The water level should be just below the basket. Add the

*Pencil asparagus are thin and cook too fast.

asparagus spears. Cover and steam for 5 minutes. Do not overcook. Carefully remove the asparagus from the steamer. While the asparagus is cooking, prepare the rest of the recipe.

Put the bread in a food processor and process until it is finely crumbed. Heat the stock to a boil. Place the bread crumbs in a bowl and add half the chicken stock, mixing well. Blend in the olive oil and add the rest of the chicken stock, the chopped egg white, parsley, white pepper, chili powder, and onion powder. Mix well. Spoon the sauce over the asparagus just before serving.

Serving size: ⅙ of recipe	Total fat: 3 grams	Dietary fiber: 2 grams
Vegetable exchanges: 2	Saturated fat: 0 grams	Sugars: 3 grams
Fat exchanges: ½	Cholesterol: 0 milligrams	Protein: 5 grams
Calories: 81	Sodium: 215 milligrams	
Calories from fat: 27	Carbohydrate: 9 grams	

Pumpernickel Dinner Rolls

YIELD: 16 small rolls

7 ounces warm water (105°–110°)
2 tablespoons molasses
2 tablespoons canola oil
1½ cups flour
¼ cup rye flour
¼ cup whole wheat flour
1 teaspoon cocoa powder
1 teaspoon gluten
1 teaspoon salt
1½ teaspoons yeast
1 teaspoon caraway seeds

Put the liquid ingredients in the baking pan of a bread machine; add all the dry ingredients in the order listed, except the yeast and caraway seeds. Level the ingredients and then add the yeast and caraway seeds. Put the baking pan into the machine. Select the dough cycle and press "start." When the dough cycle is complete, remove dough and shape it into a ball on a lightly floured surface. Divide the dough into quarters. Cut each quarter into 4 pieces. Shape each piece into a ball. Place the rolls about 2 inches apart on a cookie sheet that has been coated with cooking spray. Cover the rolls and let them rise until double in bulk, about 45 minutes to an hour.

Preheat the oven to 375° and bake the rolls for 25 to 30 minutes.

Serving size: 1 roll	Total fat: 2 grams	Carbohydrate: 14 grams
Starch exchanges: 1	Saturated fat: 0 grams	Dietary fiber: 1 gram
Calories: 80	Cholesterol: 0 milligrams	Sugars: 2 grams
Calories from fat: 17	Sodium: 148 milligrams	Protein: 2 grams

Easter Orange Cheesecake

YIELD: 1 8-inch cheesecake

⅔ cup (2½ ounces) crushed vanilla wafers
2 tablespoons butter, melted
24 ounces low-fat cream cheese
½ cup Splenda (sugar substitute)
1 teaspoon vanilla extract
¼ cup orange juice

1 tablespoon grated orange zest
4 eggs
¼ cup low-fat sour cream
¾ cup (5 ounces) canned mandarin oranges, drained
Cool Whip Lite whipped topping (optional)

Preheat the oven to 300°.

Crush the vanilla wafers with a rolling pin. Combine with melted butter. Spray an 8-inch round cake pan with cooking spray. Press the crumbs evenly into the sprayed pan. Freeze for at least 15 minutes to set.

Place the cream cheese and Splenda in the bowl of an electric mixer fitted with the paddle attachment and beat, at medium speed, until creamy, scraping the batter down from the sides of the bowl. Add the vanilla, orange juice, and zest. Beat until smooth, scraping down the sides of the bowl. With the mixer still on medium speed, add the eggs one at a time, scraping down after each addition. Mix until smooth. Add the sour cream and mix until smooth. Pour about a fourth of the mixture evenly into the pan. Distribute the orange segments over the batter, and then fill the pan with the remaining batter. Place the pan on a cookie sheet with sides in the oven and fill the cookie sheet with water. Bake for 1 hour and 10 minutes. The cheesecake will feel firm to the touch when done.

Let the cake rest 1 hour at room temperature, then chill for 3 hours before removing it from the pan. To remove the cake from the pan, place the pan directly over low heat on the range. Move it in a circular motion for 15 to 20 seconds. Place a plastic-covered plate over the pan. Press tightly and turn over, tapping the bottom of the pan to release the cake. Place the serving plate against bottom of cake and turn it back over. Top each slice with the whipped topping and 1 orange segment if desired.

Serving size: ¹⁄₁₂ cheesecake	Calories from fat: 140	Sodium: 236 milligrams
	Total fat: 16 grams	Carbohydrate: 11 grams
Starch exchanges: 1	Saturated fat: 9 grams	Dietary fiber: 0 grams
Fat exchanges: 3	Cholesterol: 110 milligrams	Sugars: 2 grams
Calories: 222		Protein: 8 grams

❧

Strawberry Chiffon Parfait

YIELD: 6 servings

Chiffon Cake

1 cup all-purpose flour
½ cup plus 1½ teaspoons Splenda (sugar substitute)
1½ teaspoons baking powder
¼ teaspoon salt
¼ cup oil

3 eggs, separated
¼ cup orange juice
2 tablespoons water
1 teaspoon vanilla extract
2 teaspoons grated orange zest
¼ teaspoon cream of tartar

Preheat the oven to 325°.

Sift together the flour, ½ cup Splenda, baking powder, and salt. Place in the bowl of an electric mixer fitted with the paddle attachment. Make a well in the center of the dry ingredients. Add the oil, egg yolks, orange juice, water, vanilla, and zest into the well and beat until smooth. In a separate bowl, whip the egg whites, cream of tartar, and 1½ teaspoons of Splenda to make a meringue. Whip until the egg whites form stiff peaks.

Take a third of the batter and gently fold it into the meringue. Then fold the meringue mixture back into the batter. Pour into an 8-inch-square pan that has been coated lightly with cooking spray. Bake 20 to 25 minutes. The cake should be lightly browned and spring back to touch. Allow to cool 30 minutes and then remove from pan.

Note: You can make the cake a day ahead if you wish.

Parfait

Chiffon cake
1½ pints of strawberries (reserve 3, cut in half for garnish)
1 tablespoon Splenda (sugar substitute)
1 cup sugar-free topping (Cool Whip Free)
6 mint leaves for garnish (if available)

Cut the cooled cake into 1-inch cubes. Clean and slice the strawberries. Puree half the strawberries in the blender and mix with the Splenda. Fold the remaining strawberries into the puree. Choose 6 glasses (stemmed wineglasses will do nicely). Put half the cake cubes evenly in the bottom of the glasses. Top with half the puree mixture. Place another layer of cake cubes in each glass and top with the remaining puree. Top each serving with whipped topping, a half strawberry, and a mint leaf.

Serving size: 1 parfait	Total fat: 7 grams	Carbohydrate: 12 grams
Starch exchanges: 1	Saturated fat: 1 gram	Dietary fiber: 1 gram
Fat exchanges: 1	Cholesterol: 62 milli-	Sugars: 2 grams
Calories: 122	grams	Protein: 3 grams
Calories from fat: 59	Sodium: 118 milligrams	

Passover

Eight days beginning on the fifteenth day of the Hebrew month Nisan, usually in March or April

*A*n important Jewish holiday, Passover celebrates the exodus of the Jews from Egypt over three thousand years ago. By escaping from Egypt, the Jews also escaped being the slaves of Pharaoh, the leader of the Egyptians. The Old Testament describes the terrible plagues God imposed on the Egyptians in order to convince them to let the Jewish people go. But Pharaoh was stubborn and would not yield. Moses, the leader of the Jewish people, foretold the final and worst plague of all: God would kill the firstborn son of every Egyptian family. The Jews, in order to be spared this plague, sacrificed a lamb to God and sprinkled some of its blood on their doorposts so that the Angel of Death would "pass over" them. This final plague frightened Pharaoh into releasing the Jews from bondage, and Moses led them out of Egypt.

Today Passover is an eight-day celebration of the "passing over" to freedom from bondage and slavery. When the Jews left Egypt, they fled quickly—so quickly that they did not have time even to let their bread dough rise! As a result they were forced to bake unleavened bread, which we know as matzo. Matzo is still eaten today during Passover in remembrance of the exodus.

A special meal called a seder is eaten on the first night of Passover. During that night the story of Moses is always read and the table is set with an extra glass of wine for Elijah, the prophet who will foretell the Messiah's coming. Special foods are always eaten, including matzo, wine—symbolizing hope for peace—bitter herbs to represent the bitterness of slavery, and greens as a reminder that Moses freed the Jews during the spring of the year. Our seder menu incorporates all these traditions, although portion sizes may need to be adjusted to accommodate the person with diabetes.

Matzo Ball Soup makes a perfect starter, as the broth is low in calories and yet quite filling, making it easier to select smaller portions of other menu items. The seder would not be complete without Gefilte Fish. Tomato-Garlic Brisket garnished with sprigs of fresh parsley and Horse-radish Sauce makes a tasty entrée. Potato Kugel and Tchatchouka, a Middle Eastern version of ratatouille, round out the menu. Honey Cake tops off this special meal.

Regardless of your religious beliefs, this is a great time of year to teach your children or grandchildren about this holiday and about the beliefs of the Jewish people. On Passover everyone can pray with the Jewish people for peace, freedom, and justice for all the people of the world.

Passover

Gefilte Fish

Matzo Ball Soup

Tomato-Garlic Brisket with Horseradish Sauce

Potato Kugel

Dilled Parsnips and Carrots

Tchatchouka

Honey Cake

Gefilte Fish

YIELD: 12 servings

Fish Stock

1 medium onion, chopped

2 stalks celery, chopped

1 medium carrot, sliced

1 bay leaf

1 teaspoon peppercorns, crushed

¼ teaspoon salt

4 cups chopped fish bones and heads

6 cups cold water

Place all the ingredients in a large pot. Bring slowly to a boil, turn the heat down, and simmer for 45 minutes. Strain, discard the solids, and put the liquid back on the stove. Bring to a boil to cook the Fish Balls (see next recipe).

Fish Balls

1½ pounds whitefish, snapper, pike,
   or cod fillets
¾ pound salmon fillets
2 small onions, chopped
½ teaspoon kosher salt
½ teaspoon ground white pepper

1 teaspoon Splenda (sugar substitute)
½ cup egg substitute
¼ cup matzo meal
Fish Stock (see previous recipe)
1 medium carrot, sliced

Grind up the fish with the chopped onions in a meat grinder. Add the salt, pepper, Splenda, and egg substitute. Blend well. Mix in the matzo meal. Blend the mixture until it gets thick enough to handle easily. If it is too thick, add a little cold water; if too thin, add a little more matzo meal. Dip a small ice cream scoop or spoon into cold water. Fill the scoop with the fish mixture and with wet hands shape the balls. Divide the mixture into a total of 12 balls.

Drop the fish balls into the boiling stock. Cover and simmer for 1½ hours. Fifteen minutes before they are done, add the carrot and finish cooking. Chill the fish balls with the stock in the refrigerator for up to 4 days. Serve with the sliced carrots and some of the stock that has now jellied.

Note: Gefilte Fish should always be chilled before serving.

Serving size: 1 fish ball	Calories from fat: 26	Sodium: 205 milligrams
Very-lean-meat	Total fat: 3 grams	Carbohydrate: 5 grams
exchanges: 2½	Saturated fat: 1 gram	Dietary fiber: 1 gram
Vegetable exchanges: 1	Cholesterol: 40 milli-	Sugars: 1 gram
Calories: 122	grams	Protein: 18 grams

Matzo Ball Soup

YIELD: 8 servings

1 tablespoon oil
½ cup egg substitute
¼ teaspoon salt
⅛ teaspoon white pepper

¼ cup matzo meal
1 teaspoon chopped fresh parsley
48 ounces Chicken Stock (see
  recipe, p. 21)

Blend together the oil and egg substitute. Add the salt and pepper. Add the matzo meal and parsley and blend just enough to incorporate. Cover and let rest in the refrigerator for 20 to 30 minutes.

Remove the mixture from the refrigerator and, using a teaspoon, measure and form 16 slightly rounded balls.

Meanwhile, bring 2 quarts of water to a boil. When the water is boiling, add the matzo balls, cover, turn the heat down, and let simmer for 20 minutes. While the matzo balls are simmering, bring the stock to a boil. Ladle 6 ounces chicken stock into each soup bowl and lift 2 cooked matzo balls out of the simmering water into each soup bowl. Serve.

Serving size: 6 ounces stock, 2 matzo balls	Calories from fat: 32	Carbohydrate: 5 grams
	Total fat: 4 grams	Dietary fiber: 0 grams
Vegetable exchanges: 1	Saturated fat: 1 gram	Sugars: 1 gram
Fat exchanges: 1	Cholesterol: 2 milligrams	Protein: 4 grams
Calories: 64	Sodium: 617 milligrams*	

*This recipe is not recommended for low-sodium diets.

Tomato-Garlic Brisket with Horseradish Sauce

YIELD: 8 servings

Brisket

3 pounds beef brisket, first cut, lean
1 tablespoon black peppercorns,
    crushed
1 onion, sliced ½ inch thick
1 carrot, sliced ½ inch thick

2 stalks celery, sliced ½ inch thick
5 cups water
3 ounces tomato paste
4 cloves garlic, minced to a paste

Preheat the oven to 325°.

Trim off any exterior fat from the brisket. With the bottom of a small pot, crush the peppercorns and rub on both sides of the brisket to season. Heat a large fry pan coated with cooking spray over high heat. Brown both sides of the brisket. Place the onion, carrot, and celery in the bottom of a roasting pan. Place the browned beef on top. Add 4 cups of water, cover, and place in the middle of the oven. Roast for 2½ to 3 hours. Using a meat thermometer, check the internal temperature of the meat periodically after 2 hours. When the temperature reaches 165°, remove the pan from the oven.

Increase the oven temperature to 375°. Mix together the tomato paste and garlic and smear this mixture over the brisket. Add another cup of water to the roasting pan if the bottom is dry. Return the pan to the oven, uncovered, for approximately 30 minutes more, or until the brisket has reached an internal temperature of 180°. Remove the pan from the oven and let the brisket rest for 20 minutes. Then slice thinly, against the grain. Reserve the juice from cooking the brisket for the Horseradish Sauce (recipe follows).

Serving size: 3 ounces	Saturated fat: 3 grams	Dietary fiber: 0 grams
Lean-meat exchanges: 3	Cholesterol: 70 milli-	Sugars: 0 grams
Calories: 177	grams	Protein: 23 grams
Calories from fat: 69	Sodium: 104 milligrams	
Total fat: 8 grams	Carbohydrate: 3 grams	

Horseradish Sauce

YIELD: 6 servings

1 cup of juice from cooking brisket
1 teaspoon cornstarch mixed with 1
teaspoon water

2–3 tablespoons prepared horseradish

Skim off any fat from the brisket juice and bring the juice to a boil. If the roast did not yield enough fat-skimmed juice, add water to bring up to 1 cup. Thicken with the cornstarch mixture and simmer slowly for 4 minutes. Take the mixture off the heat and add the prepared horseradish. Stir and serve on the side.

Serving size: 3 table-spoons	Total fat: 0 grams	Dietary fiber: 0 grams
Free food	Saturated fat: 0 grams	Sugars: 0 grams
Calories: 13	Cholesterol: 0 milligrams	Protein: 1 gram
Calories from fat: 0	Sodium: 117 milligrams	
	Carbohydrate: 2 grams	

Potato Kugel

YIELD: 6 servings

1¼ pounds of baking potatoes,
peeled
1 medium onion, thinly sliced
2 teaspoons olive oil
½ cup egg substitute, beaten

3 tablespoons matzo meal
1 teaspoon salt
½ teaspoon white pepper
½ teaspoon garlic powder

Preheat the oven to 375° and coat a 9-inch baking dish with cooking spray.

Grate the potatoes using the large holes on a grater and then mix quickly and thoroughly with all the other ingredients. Pour into the prepared baking dish. Smooth out to ensure even thickness. Bake for 50 minutes, or until browned on top. Take the kugel out of oven and let it rest for 5 minutes before serving.

Serving size: ⅙ recipe, approximately ¾ cup	Calories from fat: 21	Carbohydrate: 20 grams
	Total fat: 2 grams	Dietary fiber: 2 grams
Starch exchanges: 1	Saturated fat: 0 grams	Sugars: 1 gram
Vegetable exchanges: 1	Cholesterol: 0 milligrams	Protein: 5 grams
Calories: 123	Sodium: 235 milligrams	

Dilled Parsnips and Carrots

YIELD: 6 servings

2 medium carrots
2 medium parsnips
2 cups water

¼ teaspoon salt
½ teaspoon dill

Wash, peel, and slice the carrots and parsnips ⅛ inch thick. Bring the water to a boil. Add the salt and dill. Add the carrots and parsnips, cover, and simmer for 3 to 5 minutes, depending on how crunchy you like your vegetables. Drain the water and serve the vegetables hot.

Serving size: ⅙ recipe, approximately ¾ cup	Total fat: 0 grams	Dietary fiber: 3 grams
	Saturated fat: 0 grams	Sugars: 1 gram
Vegetable exchanges: 2	Cholesterol: 0 milligrams	Protein: 1 gram
Calories: 52	Sodium: 112 milligrams	
Calories from fat: 0	Carbohydrate: 13 grams	

Tchatchouka

YIELD: 8 servings

1 cup eggplant
2 teaspoons olive oil
1 medium onion, sliced
3 cloves garlic, chopped small
1 cup zucchini, cut into ½-inch cubes
½ cup green pepper, seeds removed, diced into ½-inch pieces

¼ teaspoon basil
¼ teaspoon oregano
⅛ teaspoon cayenne pepper
¼ teaspoon thyme
Pinch of allspice
1 15-ounce can diced tomatoes, with juice

Preheat the oven to 375°.

Peel and cut the eggplant into ½-inch cubes. Place the cubes in a bowl and sprinkle them lightly with salt. Set aside. Heat the olive oil in a 4-quart pot and sauté the onion and garlic for 2 minutes. Add the zucchini, peppers, and eggplant. Stir in the spices and mix well. Add the tomatoes with the juice. Bring to a boil, cover, and cook in the oven for 30 minutes.

Serving size: ⅛ recipe, approximately ¾ cup	Total fat: 1 gram	Dietary fiber: 3 grams
Vegetable exchanges: 2	Saturated fat: 0 grams	Sugars: 3 grams
Calories: 48	Cholesterol: 0 milligrams	Protein: 2 grams
Calories from fat: 12	Sodium: 213 milligrams	
	Carbohydrate: 9 grams	

Honey Cake

YIELD: 1 10-inch Bundt cake

⅓ cup matzo meal
⅓ cup potato starch
½ cup Splenda (sugar substitute)
¾ teaspoon cinnamon

¼ teaspoon nutmeg
8 eggs, separated
¼ cup vegetable oil
¾ cup honey

Preheat the oven to 325°.

Combine the matzo meal, potato starch, Splenda, cinnamon, and nutmeg in a large mixing bowl. Make a well in the center of the dry ingredients. Place the egg yolks in the well and beat them in with a rubber spatula. Add the oil and honey and beat until smooth. Put the egg whites in a separate bowl and use an electric mixer to whip them until they're stiff and shiny. Gently fold a third of the egg whites into the matzo mixture. Then fold in the remaining whites. Combine thoroughly, but do not overmix. Prepare a 10-inch Bundt pan with cooking spray and pour the batter into the well-sprayed pan. Bake for 1 hour. When the cake is ready, a cake tester inserted in the center will come out clean and the cake will be golden brown on top.

Note: This cake will rise to the top of the pan but settle back down about a third of the way. Allow it to cool in the pan for 15 minutes and then turn it out onto a serving plate.

Serving size: ⅟₁₆ of cake	Total fat: 6 grams	Carbohydrate: 17 grams
Starch exchanges: 1	Saturated fat: 1 gram	Dietary fiber: 0 grams
Fat exchanges: 1	Cholesterol: 106 milligrams	Sugars: 13 grams
Calories: 132	Sodium: 34 milligrams	Protein: 3 grams
Calories from fat: 54		

May

Cinco de Mayo
Mother's Day
Memorial Day

Cinco de Mayo

May 5

The Fifth of May is sometimes confused with Mexican Independence Day (which is really September 16, 1810, when the Mexicans declared their independence from Spain). The Fifth of May actually celebrates the victory of the Mexican army over Napoleon III's forces at Puebla, Mexico, in 1862.

Toward the end of 1861, when the American Civil War was raging, France, Spain, and England sent troops to Mexico to collect debts owed to their respective governments. The English and Spanish negotiated their debt repayments and quickly returned home. The French had different ideas. At the beginning of this war, an optimistic Napoleon sent Maximilian to rule Mexico because he was sure the French could conquer the Mexicans.

Cinco de Mayo was the day that an outnumbered Mexican army outmaneuvered the French and won a major battle. The War in Mexico continued and affected the Civil War, as the French were unable to send any supplies to the Confederate army because they were too busy defending themselves in Mexico. The United States was also interested in defeating the French, so after the Civil War ended, the government encouraged discharged troops to go to Mexico and join the battle against the French, who were ultimately defeated in 1867. Even though it took several years to end the war, the victory started with winning the Battle of Puebla on the Fifth of May. This celebration is a tribute to the unity, patriotism, and spirit of the Mexican people.

It's a great day for a party. If you are entertaining children, be sure to make or buy a piñata. If you decide to make your own, go to your local library or to the Internet for directions. You can fill it with your own goodies. Blindfold the children one at a time and let them take turns trying to hit the piñata with a stick to break it open. This really is best done outdoors or in a large area where you have plenty of room and can keep the rest of the children at a safe distance from the piñata and the child with the stick. Dancing is a terrific party activity for adults. Make sure you have lively music to encourage your guests to burn off calories. Diabetes is very prevalent among Mexican Americans, and in many instances it is related to overweight and a sedentary lifestyle. So use your creativity to cut calories from your recipes and engage your family in physical activity.

There are lots of delicious Mexican foods, and as you can see from our menu, they're not deep-fried!

You might want to consider serving these foods buffet style. There is lots of variety, so your guests can choose the specific foods and the amounts of those foods they want to eat. Just add mariachi music—and celebrate!

Cinco de Mayo

Baked Chips with Salsa Cruda

Mazatlán Seafood Cocktail

Nopalitos Salad

Red Snapper Veracruz

or

Chicken Enchiladas

Zesty Black Beans and Tofu

Kahlúa Parfait

or

Mexican Wedding Cookies

Baked Chips with Salsa Cruda

YIELD: 4 servings

8 6-inch corn tortillas (purchased)   Salsa Cruda (recipe follows)

Preheat the oven to 400°.

With a sharp knife, cut corn tortillas into 8 wedges, as you would slice a pizza. Lay the wedges flat on a baking sheet that has been coated with cooking spray. Bake them for 6 to 8 minutes, until lightly browned, being careful not to burn them. The chips on the outer edges of the sheet may cook faster. If so, remove them with a spatula and continue to bake the rest.

Serving size: 16 chips	Total fat: 1 gram	Carbohydrate: 24 grams
Starch exchanges: 1½	Saturated fat: 0 grams	Dietary fiber: 3 grams
Calories: 115	Cholesterol: 0 milligrams	Sugars: 0 grams
Calories from fat: 12	Sodium: 84 milligrams	Protein: 3 grams

Salsa Cruda

YIELD: About 3 cups

1–2 jalapeño peppers (optional)   1 small green pepper, diced small
3 tomatoes, chopped   2 tablespoons chopped cilantro
1 medium onion, chopped   1 teaspoon salt (optional)
1 small red pepper, diced small   2 tablespoons lime juice

Depending on how hot you like your salsa, take one or more jalapeño peppers, cut in half, and discard the seeds. Slice the pepper thin. (If you like your salsa mild, leave the jalapeño pepper out entirely.) Mix the remaining ingredients with the jalapeños. Take half of the mixture and blend smooth in a blender or food processor. Add back to remaining mixture and refrigerate. Serve with Baked Chips.

Serving size: ½ cup	Saturated fat: 0 grams	Dietary fiber: 2 grams
Vegetable exchanges: 1	Cholesterol: 0 milligrams	Sugars: 3 grams
Calories: 30	Sodium: 395 (7)* milli-	Protein: 1 gram
Calories from fat: 0	grams	
Total fat: 0 grams	Carbohydrate: 7 grams	

*Figure in parentheses does not include salt.

Mazatlán Seafood Cocktail

YIELD: 4 servings

6 small shrimp, peeled, deveined, and cut into quarters
2 ounces bay scallops
2 ounces red snapper, cut into ½-inch pieces
¼ cup lime juice
1 tablespoon onion chopped small
1 teaspoon minced garlic
1 small jalapeño pepper, sliced, seeds removed
2 tablespoons tomato, seeded and chopped small
1 tablespoon fresh chopped cilantro
2 cups lettuce sliced very thin

Bring 2 cups of water to a boil over high heat. Add the shrimp and scallops and boil for 1 minute. Add the snapper and continue to cook for 3 more minutes with water just at the boiling point. Remove from heat, drain, and chill well.

Mix the scallops, shrimp, and snapper with the lime juice, onion, garlic and jalapeño. Add the tomato and cilantro. Divide into 4 servings and serve on small plates or in margarita glasses on shredded lettuce.

Serving size: ¼ recipe	Calories from fat: 10	Sodium: 98 milligrams
Vegetable exchanges: 1	Total fat: 1 gram	Carbohydrate: 3 grams
Very-lean-meat	Saturated fat: 0 grams	Dietary fiber: 1 gram
exchanges: 1	Cholesterol: 31 milli-	Sugars: 1 gram
Calories: 57	grams	Protein: 9 grams

Nopalitos Salad

YIELD: 4 servings

Dressing

1 tablespoon Dijon mustard
2 tablespoons red wine vinegar
4 tablespoons canola oil

½ teaspoon Equal (1½ packets)
1 tablespoon water

Blend all ingredients.

Salad

2 large tomatoes, each cut into 6 thin slices
1 medium green pepper, halved, seeded, and cut into strips
1 cup canned nopales strips, drained and rinsed
1 medium onion, cut into strips

2 tablespoons minced cilantro
1 green onion, green part thinly sliced
Freshly ground black pepper
1 lime, cut into 8 wedges
½ batch dressing (recipe above)

In the center of 4 plates, lay flat 3 tomato slices. Divide the peppers, nopales, and onions into 4 equal portions. Place one portion of each on top of the tomato slices, arranging them so that they look like the spokes of a wheel. Sprinkle the tomato slices with the cilantro, green onions, and a few grindings of black pepper. Garnish each plate with 2 lime wedges. Drizzle with 1 tablespoon of dressing.

Serving size: ¼ recipe	Total fat: 3 grams	Dietary fiber: 3 grams
Vegetable exchanges: 2	Saturated fat: 0 grams	Sugars: 3 grams
Fat exchanges: ½	Cholesterol: 0 milligrams	Protein: 1 gram
Calories: 72	Sodium: 104 milligrams	
Calories from fat: 28	Carbohydrate: 11 grams	

Red Snapper Veracruz

YIELD: 4 servings

1 pound skinless, boneless red snapper, cod, or orange roughy
1 medium onion, sliced
1 clove garlic, minced
1 medium green pepper, sliced into
strips

2 medium ripe tomatoes, cut into
strips
1 tablespoon cilantro, chopped
¼ cup dry white wine (or water)
½ teaspoon lemon pepper

If the fish is frozen, defrost in refrigerator overnight.

Cut the fish into 4 portions and set aside. Heat a large nonstick sauté pan or skillet, coat it with cooking spray, add the onions and garlic, and cook over medium heat for 3 minutes. Add the pepper strips and cook for 3 more minutes. Add the tomatoes, cilantro, white wine, and lemon pepper. Bring this mixture to a boil, add the fish, and cover tightly. Turn the heat down to low and simmer for approximately 10 minutes.

Place the fish on 4 plates and spoon the sauce over it. Serve with steamed rice.

Serving size: ¼ of recipe	Total fat: 3 grams	Dietary fiber: 2 grams
Very-lean-meat exchanges: 3	Saturated fat: 1 gram	Sugars: 4 grams
Vegetable exchanges: 2	Cholesterol: 41 milli- grams	Protein: 25 grams
Calories: 161*	Sodium: 125 milligrams	Alcohol: 1 gram*
Calories from fat: 24	Carbohydrate: 8 grams	

*If you use water instead of wine, you will save 10 calories and 1 gram of alcohol per serv-
ing.

Chicken Enchiladas

YIELD: 6 servings

1½ cups cooked and shredded
    chicken
2 tablespoons onion, diced into
    ¼-inch pieces
1 teaspoon minced garlic
¼ cup green pepper, diced into
    ¼-inch pieces
½ cup tomato, diced into ¼-inch
    pieces

1¾ cups Enchilada Sauce (recipe
    follows)
¼ cup water
6 6-inch corn tortillas
¾ cup shredded low-fat mozzarella
    cheese

Preheat the oven to 400°.

In a 2-quart pot, place the chicken, onion, garlic, pepper, tomato, ¼ cup of the Enchilada Sauce, and water. Bring to a boil over high heat, then turn the heat down to medium-low, cover, and simmer for 15 minutes, or until mixture is almost dry.

Spoon ½ cup of the Enchilada Sauce on the bottom of an 8-inch square baking dish. Steam or heat the tortillas in the microwave one at a time to soften. Place ⅓ cup of the chicken mixture at one end of a softened tortilla and roll. Place the tortilla in the pan seam side down. Repeat with the remaining mixture and tortillas. Top with the remainder of the Enchilada Sauce and sprinkle with the mozzarella. Cover and bake for 15 minutes.

Serving size: 1 enchilada	Calories from fat: 52	Carbohydrate: 21 grams
Starch exchanges: 1	Total fat: 6 grams	Dietary fiber: 3 grams
Vegetable exchanges: 1	Saturated fat: 1 gram	Sugars: 3 grams
Medium-fat-meat	Cholesterol: 29 milli-	Protein: 13 grams
exchanges: 1	grams	
Calories: 179	Sodium: 264 milligrams	

Enchilada Sauce

YIELD: 6 servings (2 cups)

1 tablespoon olive oil
4 teaspoons minced onion
1 teaspoon minced garlic
2 tablespoons chili powder
¼ teaspoon cumin

1 15-ounce can tomatoes, with juice
2 tablespoons tomato paste
½ cup water
1 teaspoon Worcestershire sauce

Heat the olive oil in a heavy saucepan. Sauté the onion and garlic in the olive oil for 1 minute over medium-high heat. Add the chili powder and cumin and stir well. Add the remaining ingredients. When this starts to boil, turn the heat down and simmer, covered, for 30 minutes. Place in a blender and puree until smooth. Cool for later use.

Serving size: 3 ounces	Total fat: 3 grams	Dietary fiber: 1 gram
Vegetable exchanges: 1	Saturated fat: 0 grams	Sugars: 2 grams
Fat exchanges: ½	Cholesterol: 0 milligrams	Protein: 1 gram
Calories: 52	Sodium: 195 milligrams	
Calories from fat: 25	Carbohydrate: 7 grams	

Zesty Black Beans and Tofu

YIELD: 10 ½-cup servings

1 package firm tofu (usually found in the produce section)
1 medium onion, diced small
1 15-ounce can low-sodium black beans

1 16-ounce jar salsa (mild or spicy, depending on your taste)
1 teaspoon freshly ground black pepper

Drain the tofu and dice it into ½-inch cubes. Heat a nonstick fry pan over medium-high heat. Add the tofu and cook until all the liquid has evaporated. Add the onion and continue to cook for 3 minutes. Add the drained black beans and the salsa. Bring to a boil and turn the heat down. Simmer for 10 minutes.

This makes a great side dish, served hot, or a dip for chips, served cold.

Serving size: ½ cup	Total fat: 1 gram	Carbohydrate: 10 grams
Vegetable exchanges: 2	Saturated fat: 0 grams	Dietary fiber: 3 grams
Calories: 57	Cholesterol: 0 milligrams	Sugars: 2 grams
Calories from fat: 11	Sodium: 399 milligrams*	Protein: 5 grams

Kahlúa Parfait

YIELD: 6 servings

½ cup egg substitute
4 teaspoons Equal (12 packets)
1 ounce Kahlúa liqueur†
1 pint Cool Whip Lite whipped
    topping

1 teaspoon coffee extract‡
2⅓ ounces semisweet baking
    chocolate

Pour the egg substitute and Equal into the bowl of an electric mixer and whip until light and fluffy. Add the Kahlúa and mix in. Fold in the Cool Whip by hand. Divide the mixture in half and add the coffee extract to one half. Set aside.

Heat the chocolate until it is melted. Using a wire whisk, add the un-flavored portion of the cream mixture about half at a time to the chocolate, beating vigorously. Be sure to incorporate all the chocolate from the sides of the bowl into the mixture. Fill parfait glasses (or wineglasses) with two

---

*This recipe is not recommended for low-sodium diets.
†You may substitute 1 teaspoon instant coffee dissolved in 1 teaspoon warm water for the Kahlúa.
‡You may substitute ½ teaspoon instant coffee dissolved in ½ teaspoon warm water for the coffee extract.

alternating layers of each flavor. Freeze the parfaits for at least 6 hours before serving.

Serving size: 4 ounces	Total fat: 7 grams	Dietary fiber: 0 grams
Starch exchanges: 1	Saturated fat: 5 grams	Sugars: 10 grams
Fat exchanges: 1	Cholesterol: 0 milligrams	Protein: 3 grams
Calories: 144*	Sodium: 37 milligrams	Alcohol: 1 gram*
Calories from fat: 62	Carbohydrate: 14 grams*	(7 calories)

Mexican Wedding Cookies

YIELD: 2 dozen cookies

½ cup unsalted butter
2½ teaspoons Equal (8 packets)
1 teaspoon vanilla extract
1 Granny Smith apple
1 cup all-purpose flour

Pinch of salt
1 cup chopped walnuts
1 egg white
Flour for marking

Preheat the oven to 350°.

Beat the butter with the Equal and vanilla until it is creamy and light. Peel, core, and grate the apple. Measure 4 tablespoons of grated apple and add it to the butter mixture. Beat in. Add the flour, salt, and walnuts. Mix well to form a coarse texture. Some of the flour will look dry, and some of the pieces will be the size of peas. Add the egg white. Mix thoroughly.

Coat a cookie sheet lightly with cooking spray. Portioning the dough out by the tablespoonful, roll it into balls and place the balls on the prepared cookie sheet, about 1 inch apart. Dip a fork into flour and press a mark into the top of each cookie. Cookies should be about ⅓ inch high. Bake for 13 to 15 minutes, until bottoms of cookies are slightly browned.

Serving size: 1 cookie	Calories from fat: 58	Sodium: 15 milligrams
Starch exchanges:	Total fat: 6 grams	Carbohydrate: 6 grams
½ bread	Saturated fat: 3 grams	Dietary fiber: 0 grams
Fat exchanges: 1	Cholesterol: 10 milli-	Sugars: 0 grams
Calories: 86	grams	Protein: 1 gram

*If you use instant coffee instead of Kahlúa, you save about 12 calories per serving, 6 to 8 from alcohol and 6 from carbohydrate. However, the flavor will not be the same.

Mother's Day

Second Sunday in May

This special holiday honors mothers everywhere. While it has been officially observed in the United States since 1914, when President Woodrow Wilson proclaimed the second Sunday in May as Mother's Day, its roots can be traced to celebrations in ancient Greece honoring Rhea, the mother of the gods.

In England, "Mothering Day" was celebrated in the 1600s on the fourth Sunday of Lent. At this time many poor people worked as servants and lived in the homes of their employers. Mothering Day was a day off, and everyone was encouraged to return home and spend time with his or her mother. The day was made festive with a mothering cake.

Julia Ward Howe, the woman who wrote the words to "The Battle Hymn of the Republic," promoted a "Mother's Day" as early as 1872. She wanted the day to be devoted to peace. In 1907, Anna Jarvis started a campaign to make Mother's Day a national holiday. She convinced her church to celebrate on the second Sunday in May, the anniversary of her mother's death. By 1911 the holiday was celebrated in almost every state of the Union.

Celebrating Mother's Day is a worldwide tradition. Australia, Belgium, Denmark, Finland, and Turkey are among the countries that celebrate on the second Sunday in May. Other countries celebrate at different times of the year. No matter what the date, it is a great way to honor mothers throughout the world.

Everyone from the smallest child up can do something special for Mother's Day. While adults tend to buy gifts, send flowers, or take Mom out to dinner, the handmade card of a three-year-old holds a special place in every mother's heart. Older children may want to give Mom a gift certificate offering to do an unwanted household chore for one whole week or once a week for a month.

Some families have a tradition of serving Mom breakfast in bed on her special day. Another alternative is to offer her a festive family brunch. Set the table with the best tablecloth or placemats and make it extra special with a fresh floral centerpiece. Our Fresh Fruit Cup Appetizer, Garden Vegetable Scramble, Seafood Frittata, homemade muffins, Banana Bread, and Strawberry Yogurt Parfait are easy enough to prepare so that *everyone* can help make this special meal for Mother.

If you have little ones and they want to prepare breakfast for Mom, try the Strawberry Yogurt Parfait first. It is a meal in itself and looks very festive in a stemmed glass. If you do not have parfait glasses, you can use water goblets. This requires no cooking and allows little ones to brag that they made it all by themselves.

Mother's Day

Fresh Fruit Cup

Garden Vegetable Scramble

or

Seafood Frittata

Blueberry-Lemon Whole Wheat Muffins

or

Raspberry Corn Muffins

or

Banana Bread

Strawberry Yogurt Parfait

Fresh Fruit Cup

YIELD: 8 servings

2 oranges
Juice of 1 lemon
1 green apple
1 banana

1 kiwi
½ cup seedless red or green grapes
½ cup blueberries or blackberries
1 teaspoon Equal (3 packets)

Cut the larger fruit into bite-size pieces. Combine all ingredients, in the order listed. Stir gently after each addition. Served chilled.

Note: Any fruit you desire or have available can be used to make a fruit cup. Always start with a *citrus* fruit; the juice will keep fruit like apples or bananas from browning. Add the most fragile fruit, like raspberries, last.

If you want a macédoine of fresh fruits (fresh fruit flavored with spirits), add ½ cup of any fruit-flavored liqueur to fruit. Refrigerate for 4 hours before serving.

Serving size: ½ cup	Total fat: 0 grams	Carbohydrate: 17 grams
Fruit exchanges: 1	Saturated fat: 0 grams	Dietary fiber: 3 grams
Calories: 65	Cholesterol: 0 milligrams	Sugars: 12 grams
Calories from fat: 3	Sodium: 1 milligram	Protein: 1 gram

Garden Vegetable Scramble

YIELD: 4 servings

2 teaspoons canola or olive oil
¼ cup onion, diced small
¼ cup tomato, diced small
¼ cup mushroom, diced small
¼ cup red pepper, diced small
¼ cup green pepper, diced small

½ cup spinach, cut into strips ¼ inch
  wide by 1 inch long
1 teaspoon white pepper
½ teaspoon salt (optional)
1 cup egg substitute

Heat an 8- or 10-inch nonstick fry pan on medium heat, add the oil and all the vegetables, and sauté for 5 to 7 minutes, or until the vegetables are tender. Sprinkle with salt and pepper. Turn the heat to medium-high and pour in the egg substitute. Keep stirring until the eggs are well scrambled. Arrange the eggs on 4 serving plates. Serve with toasted whole-grain bread—no butter, of course—and a dish of fresh fruit.

Serving size: ¼ recipe	Total fat: 3 grams	Carbohydrate: 4 grams
Vegetable exchanges: 1	Saturated fat: 0 grams	Dietary fiber: 1 gram
Fat exchanges: ½	Cholesterol: 0 milligrams	Sugars: 1 gram
Calories: 50	Sodium: 324 (33)* milli-	Protein: 3 grams
Calories from fat: 27	grams	

*Figure in parentheses does not include salt.

Seafood Frittata

YIELD: 4 servings

¼ cup salmon, cut into ½-inch cubes
¼ cup whitefish, snapper, or orange roughy, cut into ½-inch cubes
6 pieces asparagus, sliced ¼ inch thick
2 teaspoons olive oil

¼ cup onion, diced small
¼ cup green pepper, diced small
¼ cup mushroom, sliced
4 pitted black olives, sliced
¼ cup baby shrimp, cooked
1 cup egg substitute

Blanch the salmon and other fish in boiling, lightly salted water for 5 minutes. Drain and set aside. Blanch the asparagus in boiling, lightly salted water for 5 minutes. Drain and set aside. Heat the olive oil in a 10-inch nonstick fry pan over medium-high heat and sauté all the vegetables for 5 minutes, or until tender. Add the blanched asparagus, olives, fish, and shrimp. Turn the heat down to medium, add the egg substitute, and mix gently. Cover, turn the heat to low, and cook for about 5 minutes, or until the mixture is firm to the touch in the center.

Slide the frittata onto a cutting board and cut it into 4 wedges. Place each wedge on a serving plate and garnish with a few slices of fresh fruit if you like.

Serving size: ¼ recipe	Total fat: 9 grams	Carbohydrate: 4 grams
Vegetable exchanges: 1	Saturated fat: 1 gram	Dietary fiber: 1 gram
Lean-meat exchanges: 3	Cholesterol: 88 milli-	Sugars: 1 gram
Calories: 200	grams	Protein: 25 grams
Calories from fat: 81	Sodium: 262 milligrams	

Blueberry-Lemon Whole Wheat Muffins

YIELD: 18 2-inch muffins

1 cup all-purpose flour
1 cup whole-grain flour
½ teaspoon salt
2¼ teaspoons baking powder
1 tablespoon Equal (10 packets)
1 egg

1¼ cups 2% milk
¼ cup canola oil
1½ teaspoons fresh lemon juice
¾ teaspoon grated lemon zest
1 cup blueberries, individually
    quick-frozen

Preheat the oven to 325°.

Reserving 1 tablespoon of the all-purpose flour to sprinkle over the berries, sift together the flours, salt, baking powder, and Equal into the bowl of an electric mixer fitted with the paddle attachment. Add the egg, milk, oil, lemon juice, and zest. Mix only until combined. Toss the 1 tablespoon of reserved flour over the berries to coat them. Using a rubber spatula, gently fold the berries into the mix. Coat the muffin pans with cooking spray or use paper muffin liners. Fill the muffin cups three-quarters full. Bake for approximately 15 minutes, or until the muffins have risen and are lightly browned.

Serving size: 1 muffin	Saturated fat: 0 grams	Dietary fiber: 1 gram
Starch exchanges: 1	Cholesterol: 12 milli-	Sugars: 2 grams
Calories: 96	grams	Protein: 3 grams
Calories from fat: 34	Sodium: 127 milligrams	
Total fat: 7 grams	Carbohydrate: 13 grams	

Raspberry Corn Muffins

YIELD: 24 2-inch muffins

1 cup cornmeal
1 cup all-purpose flour
¼ teaspoon salt
1 tablespoon baking powder
2 tablespoons Splenda (sugar substitute)

1 egg
2 tablespoons canola oil
¾ cup 2% milk
¼ cup sour cream
¾ cup fresh raspberries

Preheat the oven to 400°.

Put the cornmeal, flour, salt, baking powder, and Splenda into the bowl of an electric mixer fitted with the paddle attachment. Mix until just combined. Add the egg, oil, milk, and sour cream. Mix until just combined. Do not overmix. Fold in the raspberries by hand, using a rubber spatula, gently, so you do not break them up. Drop by overfilled tablespoonsful into muffin pans that are either coated with cooking spray or lined with paper muffin cups. Bake 10 to 12 minutes, until muffins are a light golden color.

Serving size: 1 muffin	Saturated fat: 1 gram	Dietary fiber: 1 gram
Starch exchanges: 1	Cholesterol: 10 milli-	Sugars: 1 gram
Calories: 68	grams	Protein: 2 grams
Calories from fat: 19	Sodium: 175 milligrams	
Total fat: 2 grams	Carbohydrate: 10 grams	

Banana Bread

YIELD: 1 loaf (9 by 5 by 3 inches), 16 slices

2 cups all-purpose flour
1 teaspoon baking soda
¼ teaspoon cinnamon
⅛ teaspoon nutmeg
3 overripe medium bananas,*
  chopped

2 eggs
¼ cup granulated sugar
¼ cup Splenda (sugar substitute)
½ cup unsweetened applesauce
1 teaspoon vanilla extract
½ cup chopped walnuts (optional)

Preheat the oven to 350°.

Sift together the flour, baking soda, cinnamon, and nutmeg into the large bowl of an electric mixer. Add all the other ingredients to the bowl and mix to combine. Do not overmix. Spray a loaf pan with cooking spray. Pour the batter into the prepared pan.

Bake approximately 1 hour. Check by inserting a toothpick in the center of the loaf. It will come out clean when the bread is done.

Serving size: 1 slice	Saturated fat: 0 grams	Dietary fiber: 1 gram
Starch exchanges: 1½	Cholesterol: 27 milli-	Sugars: 9 grams
Calories: 134 (112)[†]	grams	Protein: 3 grams
Calories from fat: 26 (8)[†]	Sodium: 88 milligrams	
Total fat: 3 (1)[†] grams	Carbohydrate: 24 grams	

*Bananas must be overripe—the riper the better! You can save overripe bananas in your freezer.
[†]Figures in parentheses indicate nutritional information if nuts are left out.

Strawberry Yogurt Parfait

YIELD: 4 servings

2 cups low-fat granola
2 cups plain or flavored low-fat, low-
   calorie yogurt

1 pint fresh strawberries or your
   favorite berries

Set out 4 parfait glasses, or choose tall, clear glasses, like a white-wine glass. Place ¼ cup of the granola in the bottom of each glass. Carefully spoon ¼ cup of the yogurt on top of each. Add 2 strawberries that have been washed and sliced. Repeat a layer of granola and one of yogurt, and then finish with the balance of the strawberries.

This must be served immediately after it is made or the yogurt will make the crunchy granola soggy.

Serving size: 1 parfait	Calories from fat: 30	Carbohydrate: 53 grams
Starch exchanges: 1	Total fat: 3 grams	Dietary fiber: 5 grams
Fruit exchanges: 2	Saturated fat: 0 grams	Sugars: 18 grams
Skim-milk exchanges: 1	Cholesterol: 2 milligrams	Protein: 10 grams
Calories: 272	Sodium: 190 milligrams	

Memorial Day

Last Monday in May

Memorial Day honors those brave men and women who gave their lives in the service of their country. This holiday was originally called Decoration Day when it originated during the Civil War, because women decorated the graves of the men who were killed in the war with flowers. Today we remember the dead of all our wars on this day.

Many families take this time to remember not only those who lost their lives serving their country but also their own deceased family members. They may take flowers and "decorate" the graves of their loved ones.

Because this holiday is always celebrated on a Monday, it is a three-day holiday for many people. Unofficially, it is considered the beginning of summer, a time for picnics, barbecues, and gatherings of family and friends. Children celebrate because the school year is nearly over, and adults look forward to a break in their daily routine. Make sure your day includes physical activity. You could go bike riding as a family, or go for a walk or run. If your celebration takes place near water, swimming is a great activity.

Our Memorial Day menu is easy on the cook. Much of it can be prepared ahead of time and grilled outdoors. Serving family-style lets guests with diabetes select the amount they want to eat. Grilled Tomatoes are a tasty way to get your veggies, and they allow all your guests to benefit from healthful choices, too. Make the Green and Red Coleslaw on the same day you plan to serve it, so it is not soggy. However, you can prepare your Parmesan Grilled Tomatoes and scrub and wrap your potatoes ahead of time. Also, prepare your meats for the grill early on, keeping them refrigerated until it's time to cook. If you plan to cook at the beach or the park, make sure you have enough cooler space to keep all perishable items cold. Bake your shortcake biscuits and prepare your strawberries before-hand.

This menu makes it easy to plan for either a small party or a large one. Plan for a half cup of coleslaw, one potato, and one Tomato for each person. The amount of meat you buy, and whether or not you serve both meats or choose one, would depend on the number of guests. Each pound of un-cooked flank steak will make four to five three-ounce servings; each half pound of ribs will yield about three ounces of cooked meat. So whether you are entertaining four or forty, you can use these recipes to help sim-plify your party and enjoy your first cookout of summer!

Memorial Day

Green and Red Coleslaw

Citrus Grilled Flank Steak

or

Country-Style Barbecued Spareribs

Parmesan Grilled Tomatoes

Grilled Baked Potatoes

Individual Ginger and Lemon Strawberry Shortcakes

or

Strawberry Rhubarb Crisp

Green and Red Coleslaw

YIELD: 8 servings

2 cups shredded green cabbage
1 cup shredded red cabbage
2 stalks celery, finely sliced
2 green onions, finely sliced

1 large carrot, shredded
¼ cup peeled and grated firm apple
  (like Granny Smith)

Dressing

½ cup low-fat mayonnaise

1 tablespoon apple cider vinegar

Place the vegetables and apple in a large mixing bowl and combine. Blend together the mayonnaise and vinegar, then stir into the vegetable mixture. Cover and chill in the refrigerator for at least 2 hours. Stir once every hour.

Serving size: ½ cup	Total fat: 1 gram	Carbohydrate: 11 grams
Vegetable exchanges: 2	Saturated fat: 0 grams	Dietary fiber: 1 gram
Calories: 54	Cholesterol: 0 milligrams	Sugars: 8 grams
Calories from fat: 10	Sodium: 155 milligrams	Protein: 1 gram

Citrus Grilled Flank Steak

YIELD: 6 servings

1 tablespoon minced garlic
2 teaspoons cumin
2 tablespoons orange juice
1 tablespoon lemon juice
1 tablespoon lime juice

2 tablespoons red wine vinegar
1 teaspoon red pepper flakes
2 tablespoons water
2 pounds flank steak, ¾ inch thick
Fresh thyme sprigs (optional)

Mix together all the ingredients, except the steak, and place in a shallow, nonreactive dish (glass or stainless steel). Coat the meat well with the mixture, cover, and marinate for at least 6 hours, turning every couple of hours. Light the grill and when it is hot, remove the steaks from the marinade. Place the steaks on the grill and sear for about 4 minutes, watching that there aren't any flare-ups. Move the steaks to a slightly different spot, away from flare-ups, if necessary. Turn them over and season to taste with salt and freshly ground black pepper. Cook for another 4 minutes, or until the meat is still slightly pink in the middle. Remove the meat from the fire and let rest for 5 minutes. Slice the steak against the grain into 1-inch-wide strips. Serve on a platter. Garnish with fresh thyme if you like.

Serving size: 4 ounces	Saturated fat: 5 grams	Dietary fiber: 0 grams
Lean-meat exchanges: 4	Cholesterol: 60 milli-	Sugars: 0 grams
Calories: 243	grams	Protein: 31 grams
Calories from fat: 112	Sodium: 86 milligrams	
Total fat: 12 grams	Carbohydrate: 0 grams	

Country-Style Barbecued Spareribs

YIELD: 6 servings

4 cups water
1 tablespoon white vinegar
2 tablespoons Worcestershire sauce
2 teaspoons Tabasco sauce
1 small onion, thinly sliced

2 pounds country-style pork ribs, trimmed of any excess fat
1 cup Barbecue Sauce (recipe follows)

Bring the water to a boil with the vinegar, Worcestershire and Tabasco sauces, and onion. Add the ribs. Cover and simmer for 45 minutes on medium-low heat. Remove the ribs from the water and place them in the refrigerator, covered, until ready to grill. (This step can be done the day before.) Create a not-too-hot fire on the grill in order to cook the ribs slowly. Coat one side of the ribs with cooking spray and place them coated side down on the grill. Keep an eye on the meat and move it if you have flare-ups. After 10 minutes turn the meat over. The ribs should be lightly browned. Cook the other side for 10 minutes. Before you turn the ribs again, brush each piece with 1 tablespoon of any barbecue sauce of your liking or the one listed here. Coat the other side and grill for about 2 minutes on each side.

Serving size: 4 ounces (⅙ recipe)	Calories: 385	Sodium: 1019 milligrams*
Medium-fat-meat exchanges: 4	Calories from fat: 223	Carbohydrate: 6 grams
Fat exchanges: 1	Total fat: 25 grams	Dietary fiber: 0 grams
Vegetable exchanges: 1	Saturated fat: 10 grams	Sugars: 3 grams
	Cholesterol: 103 milligrams	Protein: 29 grams

*This recipe is not recommended for low-sodium diets.

Barbecue Sauce

YIELD: 2 cups

1 clove garlic, finely minced
½ teaspoon sesame oil
1 cup low-sodium tamari soy sauce
1 cup water
2 tablespoons Splenda (sugar substitute)

2 tablespoons hoisin sauce
1 tablespoon cornstarch mixed with
  1 tablespoon water
1 green onion, finely chopped

Sauté the garlic in the oil for 2 minutes. Add the tamari, water, Splenda, and hoisin sauce. Bring to a boil. Reduce the heat and simmer for 2 minutes. Thicken with the cornstarch mixture and continue to simmer for 2 minutes. Add the green onion and take off stove. This sauce can be made ahead of time and refrigerated for up to 3 days.

Serving size: 2 tablespoons	Total fat: 0 grams	Dietary fiber: 0 grams
Free food	Saturated fat: 0 grams	Sugars: 2 grams
Calories: 18	Cholesterol: 0 milligrams	Protein: 1 gram
Calories from fat: 2	Sodium: 633 milligrams*	
	Carbohydrate: 3 grams	

*This recipe is not recommended for low-sodium diets.

Parmesan Grilled Tomatoes

YIELD: **6 servings**

3 tomatoes, each about 2½ inches in
    diameter
Pinch of salt
Pinch of freshly ground black pepper
6 tablespoons grated Parmesan
    cheese

¾ teaspoon basil
¾ teaspoon oregano
1½ teaspoons parsley flakes
1 tablespoon olive oil

Preheat the grill until it is hot.

Wash the tomatoes and cut them in half across the center. Place cut side up on a platter and sprinkle each half with salt and pepper.

Mix together the grated cheese, basil, oregano, and parsley. Distribute this mixture evenly over the cut side of the tomatoes. Lightly coat an 8-by-6-inch piece of foil with the olive oil. Place the foil on the hot grill and then arrange the tomatoes evenly spaced on the foil. Grill 13 to 15 minutes with the lid of the grill closed. Test with a fork for doneness; the tomatoes will feel soft when done.

Serving size: ½ tomato	Total fat: 4 grams	Carbohydrate: 1 gram
Fat exchanges: 1	Saturated fat: 1 gram	Dietary fiber: 0 grams
Calories: 48	Cholesterol: 4 milligrams	Sugars: 1 gram
Calories from fat: 35	Sodium: 134 milligrams	Protein: 2 grams

Grilled Baked Potatoes

YIELD: 6 servings

3 medium baking potatoes
1 tablespoon olive oil
1½ teaspoons Mrs. Dash Seasoning

½ cup nonfat sour cream
1 tablespoon dried chives

Bake the potatoes for 45 minutes at 400°. Cool them at room temperature for 30 minutes, then refrigerate.

Note: The potatoes should be baked a day ahead of time, or at least 4 hours before grilling.

Preheat the grill until it is hot.

Cut the cooled potatoes in half lengthwise. Rub each cut side with ½ teaspoon of the olive oil and sprinkle seasoning evenly over each half. Place the potatoes on the grill and grill the uncut side for 10 minutes. Turn them over and grill 10 minutes on the cut side. Remove the potatoes from the grill. Top each with a generous tablespoon of nonfat sour cream and sprinkle with chives.

Serving size: ½ potato	Total fat: 2 grams	Carbohydrate: 30 grams
Starch exchanges: 2	Saturated fat: 0 grams	Dietary fiber: 2 grams
Calories: 154	Cholesterol: 0 milligrams	Sugars: 3 grams
Calories from fat: 21	Sodium: 25 milligrams	Protein: 4 grams

Individual Ginger and Lemon Strawberry Shortcakes

YIELD: 6 servings

1½ pints fresh strawberries
½ teaspoon Equal (1½ packets)
4 tablespoons unsalted butter
2 tablespoons granulated sugar
1 cup all-purpose flour
1 teaspoon baking powder
1 teaspoon ground ginger

⅛ teaspoon salt
½ teaspoon grated lemon zest
½ teaspoon fresh lemon juice
4 ounces buttermilk
1½ cups Cool Whip Lite whipped
  topping

Preheat the oven to 350°.

Wash the strawberries and cut them in quarters. Divide the berries in half. Sprinkle half with the Equal. Put the other half into a food processor fitted with the steel blade and puree. Stir the puree into the cut strawberries, cover, and refrigerate.

To make the shortcakes, using an electric mixer, beat the butter and sugar until light and creamy. Sift together the flour, baking powder, ginger, and salt. Attach the dough hook to the mixer, or use a dough blender or fork, and cut the dry ingredients into the butter and sugar. Blend until pieces are the size of peas. Add the lemon zest, lemon juice, and 2 ounces of the buttermilk. Mix until just combined. Do not overmix.

Turn the dough out onto a floured pastry board. Knead by hand 2 or 3 times. Roll out to ½ inch thick. Cut out circles with a 2½-inch biscuit cutter. Spray a cookie sheet lightly with cooking spray and arrange the shortcakes on it 1½ inches apart. Use a pastry brush to brush the shortcakes with the remaining buttermilk. Bake for 12 to 15 minutes, until light brown. Cool.

Assemble the dessert immediately before serving. Cut each shortcake in half, place the bottom halves on individual dessert plates, and cover them with the berry mixture, dividing it evenly. Cover the berries with the whipped topping and then place the other half of the shortcake on top.

Serving size: ⅙ recipe	Total fat: 10 grams	Carbohydrate: 31 grams
Starch exchanges: 2	Saturated fat: 7 grams	Dietary fiber: 2 grams
Fat exchanges: 2	Cholesterol: 22 milli-	Sugars: 11 grams
Calories: 232	grams	Protein: 4 grams
Calories from fat: 93	Sodium: 130 milligrams	

Strawberry Rhubarb Crisp

YIELD: 8 servings

1¼ pounds rhubarb
1 small orange
1 tablespoon dark rum or 1 teaspoon
    rum extract
¼ cup sugar
1 pint fresh strawberries, cut into
    quarters

¾ teaspoon Equal (4 packets)
4 tablespoons unsalted butter
1 teaspoon salt
½ cup brown sugar
¾ cup all-purpose flour

Preheat the oven to 450°.

Wash the rhubarb thoroughly. Trim the ends and peel, as you would celery stalks, then cut into ¼-inch slices. Zest the skin off the orange with a fine grater, then squeeze the juice from the orange and strain it. Put the rhubarb, zest, juice, rum or extract, and sugar into a saucepan with a heavy bottom. Cook over medium heat, covered, stirring occasionally, approximately 10 minutes, or until rhubarb is al dente. Remove from heat.

Puree ½ cup of the strawberries in a blender to make ¼ cup of puree. Fold the puree, the remaining strawberries, and the Equal together. Combine the rhubarb and the strawberry mixture. Divide into 8 individual ovenproof dishes.

Chop the butter into ¼-inch pieces, place in the bowl of an electric mixer fitted with the paddle attachment, and add all the remaining ingredients. Mix on low speed to form a crumbly topping. Do not overmix. The topping should have a rough texture, with pieces the size of peas. Cover the tops of the filled dishes generously with about ⅓ inch of topping. Place the dishes on a cookie sheet in preheated oven. Bake approximately 10 minutes, or until topping is brown and crunchy. Cool about 5 minutes and serve.

Serving size: ⅛ recipe	Total fat: 6 grams	Carbohydrate: 30 grams
Starch exchanges: 2	Saturated fat: 4 grams	Dietary fiber: 2 grams
Fat exchanges: 1	Cholesterol: 16 milli-	Sugars: 17 grams
Calories: 178	grams	Protein: 2 grams
Calories from fat: 54	Sodium: 249 milligrams	

June

Father's Day

Father's Day

Third Sunday in June

*L*egend tells us that this day, one meant to honor fathers everywhere, originated when a woman named Sonora Smart Dodd was in church listening to a Mother's Day sermon in 1909. Years earlier her mother had died, leaving six small children. Her father, William Jackson Smart, raised the children alone. Sonora thought it was only fair to show the same honor and respect for fathers as was being given to mothers. She organized the first Father's Day Celebration in Spokane, Washington, on June 19, 1910.

Harry C. Meek was another early supporter of setting aside a special day to honor fathers. He was recognized in 1920 by the Lions Club as the "Originator of Father's Day." Regardless of who had the original idea, the concept caught on, and a National Father's Day Committee was formed in New York City in 1926.

President Calvin Coolidge supported the idea as early as 1924. However, it wasn't until more than thirty years later, in 1956, that Congress passed a joint resolution supporting this holiday. And finally, ten years after that, in 1966, that President Lyndon Johnson officially declared the third Sunday in June as "Father's Day."

It is a great day to honor your dad, your grandfather, or any man who has in some way served as a father to you. Perhaps you can treat him to his favorite sport. If your dad is a golfer, give him a round of golf as a great gift. Encourage him to walk the eighteen holes, just as the pros do. That exercise is a good way to start his special day.

Cook dinner inside, so Dad doesn't get stuck doing the grilling. Our menu is fit for a king, and if your father has diabetes, most likely it will "fit" his meal plan as well. Beef tenderloin is naturally lean, and if the Chocolate Mousse or Coconut Custard Pie exceeds his limits for the meal, save it for a snack later in the day. Make your dinner special, with festive tableware and a spring centerpiece. Dad will appreciate anything you do for him.

Father's Day

Spicy Corn and Black Bean Salad

Beef Bordelaise

Green Beans with Red Pepper Sauté

Roasted Rosemary Potato Wedges

Chocolate Mousse

or

Coconut Custard Pie

Spicy Corn and Black Bean Salad

YIELD: 6 servings

1 cup frozen corn, defrosted
1 cup canned black beans, drained
and rinsed
¼ cup finely diced green pepper
¼ cup finely diced red pepper
1 tablespoon seeded and finely diced
jalapeño pepper
1 tablespoon finely chopped cilantro

¼ cup finely diced red onion
2 tablespoons olive oil
2 tablespoons rice wine vinegar
1 teaspoon Splenda (sugar substitute)
2 teaspoons Dijon mustard
¼ teaspoon salt
2 teaspoons water
6 lettuce leaves

In a large bowl, mix the corn, beans, peppers, cilantro, and onions, until completely combined. In a separate small bowl, blend the olive oil, vinegar, Splenda, mustard, salt, and water. Combine and toss. Serve well chilled, atop chilled plates lined with lettuce leaves.

Serving size: ½ cup	Total fat: 5 grams	Dietary fiber: 3 grams
Vegetable exchanges: 2	Saturated fat: 0 grams	Sugars: 1 gram
Fat exchanges: 1	Cholesterol: 0 milligrams	Protein: 1 gram
Calories: 90	Sodium: 262 milligrams	
Calories from fat: 42	Carbohydrate: 11 grams	

Beef Bordelaise

YIELD: 6 servings

Beef Tenderloin

2 pounds beef tenderloin, center cut
1 teaspoon salt (optional)
2 teaspoons freshly ground black
   pepper

2 teaspoons chopped fresh rosemary

Preheat the oven to 300°.

Dry the beef with a paper towel. Rub salt, pepper, and rosemary on all sides. Heat a nonstick fry pan, with an ovenproof handle large enough to fit the beef, on high heat. Lightly brown the beef on all sides, then remove the pan from the stove and place it in the oven. Roast the beef for about 30 to 60 minutes, depending on how you like your meat done. Start checking for doneness at 30 minutes by inserting the tip of a meat thermometer into the very center of the roast. The following temperatures should serve as a guideline: rare: 120°; medium rare: 128°; medium: 135°; medium-well: 145°; well done: 155°.

When the roast is done to your liking, remove it from the pan and wrap loosely in foil. Set aside at least 20 minutes before carving.

Serving size: 4 ounces	Saturated fat: 4 grams	Carbohydrate: 0 grams
Lean-meat exchanges: 4	Cholesterol: 94 milli-	Dietary fiber: 0 grams
Calories: 241	grams	Sugars: 0 grams
Calories from fat: 105	Sodium: 457 (59)* milli-	Protein: 31 grams
Total fat: 12 grams	grams	

Bordelaise Sauce

1 small onion, sliced
1 small carrot, sliced
1 stalk celery, sliced
1 tablespoon canola oil
2 tablespoons tomato paste
2 tablespoons flour

½ cup dry red wine (optional)
2 cups Beef Stock (recipe follows)
1 bay leaf
1 teaspoon finely chopped fresh
    rosemary

Heat a 2-quart pot on high heat. Sauté the vegetables in the oil until lightly brown. Add the tomato paste and flour and continue to stir with a wooden spoon for about 2 minutes. Scrape the bottom often so the flour does not burn or stick and is well mixed with the vegetables. Turn heat down to medium and add the wine (½ cup of water if you do not want to use wine). Mix well. Add the stock and bay leaf and simmer for 30 minutes. Strain and return the sauce to the stove and continue cooking until sauce is reduced to 1 cup, about 10 to 15 minutes. Finish the sauce with a few grindings of black pepper and fresh rosemary. This sauce should be smooth, dark brown, and slightly thick.

Serving size: 1½ table-	Total fat: 3 grams	Dietary fiber: 0 grams
spoons	Saturated fat: 0 grams	Sugars: 1 gram
Vegetable exchanges: 1	Cholesterol: 0 milligrams	Protein: 2 grams
Calories: 48 (55)†	Sodium: 221 milligrams	Alcohol: (1)† gram
Calories from fat: 24	Carbohydrate: 4 grams	

*Figure in parentheses does not include salt.
†Figures in parentheses are for wine included in preparation.

Beef Stock

YIELD: 1 quart (4 cups)

2 pounds beef bones, cut into small pieces (shank or leg bones are best)

2 medium carrots, washed, coarsely chopped

1 medium onion, not peeled, quartered

2 cloves garlic, cut in half

1 stalk celery, coarsely chopped

2 tomatoes, quartered

1 teaspoon thyme

1 teaspoon rosemary

1 tablespoon peppercorns

1 teaspoon salt (optional)

1 bay leaf

12 cups cold water

Preheat the oven to 450°.

Brown the bones in a roasting pan for 15 minutes. Stir. Add the vegetables and cook for 15 minutes more. Remove from oven and transfer the contents of the baking pan into a large pot. Add the seasonings and cold water. Start with medium heat and bring the stock up to a boil. Turn the heat down to low and simmer gently for 3 hours. Skim off any scum or fat that rises to the surface.

Strain the stock through a fine mesh strainer. Discard the bones and vegetables. There should be about 1 quart of liquid left. If you have more, put the stock back on the stove and gently reduce to 1 quart. Place the stock in the refrigerator and let it cool for 6 to 8 hours or overnight. When cold, the fat will be hardened and can be easily lifted from the top.

The stock will keep for 1 week covered in the refrigerator or for several months if frozen.

Note: Freeze any remaining stock in small containers for use in other recipes.

Serving size: ½ cup	Saturated fat: 2 grams	Dietary fiber: 0 grams
Free food	Cholesterol: 0 milligrams	Sugars: 0 grams
Calories: 14	Sodium: 319 (28)* milli-	Protein: 2 grams
Calories from fat: 4	grams	
Total fat: 0 grams	Carbohydrate: 0 grams	

*Figure in parentheses does not include salt.

Green Beans with Red Pepper Sauté

YIELD: 6 servings

¾ pound green beans, cut into
   1–1½-inch lengths
1 teaspoon olive oil
½ medium onion cut into strips 1
   inch long

1 clove garlic, minced
1 medium red pepper cut into strips
   1 inch long
Salt and pepper to taste

Boil the beans for 8 to 9 minutes in 3 cups of water. While the beans are cooking, heat the olive oil in a nonstick fry pan over medium heat, add the onions and garlic, and sauté for 2 minutes. Add the peppers and continue to sauté, tossing or stirring often. When the beans are done, drain them and add them to the fry pan. Season with salt and pepper if desired and stir or toss well. Remove from heat and serve.

Serving size: ½ cup	Total fat: 1 gram	Carbohydrate: 5 grams
Vegetable exchanges: 1	Saturated fat: 0 grams	Dietary fiber: 2 grams
Calories: 37	Cholesterol: 0 milligrams	Sugars: 2 grams
Calories from fat: 8	Sodium: 4 milligrams	Protein: 1 gram

Roasted Rosemary Potato Wedges

YIELD: 4 servings

3 baking potatoes, washed
1 tablespoon fresh rosemary leaves
    pulled from stem
¼ teaspoon salt

½ teaspoon freshly ground black
    pepper
1 teaspoon paprika

Preheat the oven to 400°.

Coat a roasting pan or cookie sheet pan with cooking spray. Cut each potato in half, then each half into 4 long, thin wedges. Mix together the rosemary, salt, pepper, and paprika in a plastic bag. Add the potatoes to the bag and toss well. Lay the potatoes flat on the baking sheet and roast for 20 minutes. Turn the potatoes over and cook them for another 20 minutes, or until golden brown and crispy.

Serving size: ¼ recipe, approximately ½ cup	Total fat: 0 grams	Dietary fiber: 2 grams
	Saturated fat: 0 grams	Sugars: 0 grams
Starch exchanges: 1	Cholesterol: 0 milligrams	Protein: 2 grams
Calories: 69	Sodium: 151 milligrams	
Calories from fat: 1	Carbohydrate: 16 grams	

Chocolate Mousse

YIELD: 6 servings

½ cup egg substitute
2 teaspoons Equal (7 packets)
6 ounces semisweet chocolate
1 pint plus ½ cup Cool Whip Lite
   whipped topping

1 ounce semisweet chocolate (optional, for garnish)

Using an electric mixer, whip the egg substitute with the Equal until light and fluffy. Melt the chocolate in the top of a double boiler. Remove the chocolate from the heat. With a wire whisk, whip the egg substitute into the chocolate. Scrape down the mixture as you beat to completely combine. Using a rubber spatula, fold 1 pint of the Cool Whip Lite into chocolate mixture. Mix gently but thoroughly. Divide into 6 parfait glasses or stemmed wineglasses. Top each serving with a generous spoonful of whipped topping.

As an added garnish, grate a small amount of some extra chocolate and sprinkle it on top of the whipped cream.

Serving size: ⅙ recipe	Total fat: 15 grams	Dietary fiber: 2 grams
Starch exchanges: 1½	Saturated fat: 9 grams	Sugars: 18 grams
Fat exchanges: 3	Cholesterol: 0 milligrams	Protein: 4 grams
Calories: 247	Sodium: 40 milligrams	
Calories from fat: 131	Carbohydrate: 25 grams	

Coconut Custard Pie

YIELD: 1 9-inch pie

2 cups 2% milk
Pinch of salt
2½ tablespoons cornstarch
1 egg
1 egg yolk (reserve the white for
    another use)
1 tablespoon butter, chopped
1 teaspoon vanilla extract

2 teaspoons Equal (7 packets)
¾ cup shredded coconut
1 9-inch pie shell, regular, prebaked
    till golden brown and cooled
    (available frozen)
1 cup Cool Whip Lite whipped top-
    ping

Bring 1½ cups of the milk and the salt to a boil in a heavy saucepan. In a separate bowl, dissolve the cornstarch in the remaining ½ cup milk, add the egg and yolk, and mix to combine. Whisk a third of the boiling milk into the cornstarch mixture using a wire whisk. Then whisk this back into the remainder of the boiling milk. Reduce heat to simmer and cook for 2 minutes, stirring constantly. Remove from heat.

Add the chopped butter and stir until it is dissolved. Add the vanilla, Equal, and coconut. Mix until completely combined. Pour into the pre-baked pie shell. Cover with plastic wrap and allow the wrap to touch the custard, to prevent a skin from forming. Chill at least 3 hours before cutting. Top each piece with a generous spoonful of whipped topping.

Serving size: ⅒ of pie	Total fat: 12 grams	Carbohydrate: 16 grams
Starch exchanges: 1	Saturated fat: 6 grams	Dietary fiber: 1 gram
Fat exchanges: 2	Cholesterol: 49 milli-	Sugars: 3 grams
Calories: 192	grams	Protein: 4 grams
Calories from fat: 110	Sodium: 157 milligrams	

July

Independence Day/Canada Day

Independence Day/
Canada Day

July 4/July 1

July is the month in which Americans and Canadians celebrate the birth of their countries.

Independence Day, or the Fourth of July, is the official birthday of the United States of America. It commemorates the signing of the Declaration of Independence by the Continental Congress on July 4, 1776, in Philadelphia, Pennsylvania.

During this era King George III of England ruled the thirteen original colonies. However, the colonists objected to taxation without representation, and they showed their anger with the Boston Tea Party in 1773. In response, King George sent troops to try to control their rebellion.

In 1774, each of the colonies sent representatives to Philadelphia to convene the First Continental Congress. There was unrest among the colonists; they were unhappy with England but not yet ready to go to war. In April 1775, the king's army advanced on Concord, Massachusetts, to suppress a colonial uprising, causing Paul Revere to embark on his famous midnight ride. The Battle of Concord that followed represented the battle for the republic, and during it "the shot heard 'round the world" was fired.

The Continental Congress tried to work out its differences with England—to no avail. By June of 1776 it became apparent that they would not succeed, and a committee was appointed to write the Declaration of Independence. On July 4, members voted to accept this document. John Hancock, president of the Continental Congress, signed the Declaration of Independence "with a great flourish" so that King George could read the signature without his spectacles. The document declaring a new country, no longer under English rule, was read to cheering crowds in Independence Square, accompanied by the pealing of the Liberty Bell.

Canada's birthday celebrates the anniversary of the British North America Act bringing Lower (Ontario and Quebec) Canada into the Dominion of Canada. Dominion Day, the original name of this holiday, was officially established in 1867. Canada has grown since that time and now includes the additional provinces of Alberta, British Columbia, Manitoba, Newfoundland, Prince Edward Island, Saskatchewan, the Northwest Territory, and the Yukon Territory.

The holiday has been celebrated annually since 1958, when flags and patriotism became part of the tradition. In 1968, multicultural celebrations started and were celebrated throughout the whole month of July. The name of this holiday was officially changed from Dominion Day to Canada Day in 1982. Today, Canada Day committees in every province and territory organize and coordinate local celebrations.

These holidays in both countries are celebrated with parades, picnics, band concerts, and fireworks. They are also an excellent day to do something physically active. Baseball, tennis, and swimming are enjoyable, sometimes competitive, and they can burn up any extra calories people might consume.

So invite your friends and neighbors over and have a celebration. The menu choices offered let your guests select a tasty meal well within their dietary parameters. Fire up the grill and enjoy a delicious day.

Independence Day/ Canada Day

Tomato Salad with Balsamic Vinaigrette

Grilled Pacific Salmon

Mango and Bourbon Chicken Breasts

Russet Burgers

Baked Beans Canadian Style

Vegetable Kabobs

Maple Walnut Brownies

Red, White, and Blueberry Chiffon Cake

Tomato Salad with Balsamic Vinaigrette

YIELD: 6 servings

Balsamic Vinaigrette

¼ cup balsamic vinegar
3 tablespoons water

2 teaspoons Dijon mustard
1 packet Sweet'N Low

Mix all the ingredients, put the vinaigrette into a tightly covered container, and chill it well in the refrigerator. This dressing can be made ahead of time (it will keep for approximately 2 weeks, if kept refrigerated).

Salad

3 medium vine-ripened tomatoes
1 small sweet onion
¼ cup fresh basil leaves, cut into
    strips

¼ teaspoon freshly ground black
    pepper

Thickly slice the tomatoes and lay them out on a platter, alternating them with the thinly sliced sweet onion. Top with basil leaves and freshly ground black pepper.

Spoon the vinaigrette over the salad just before serving.

Serving size: ⅙ of recipe	Total fat: ½ gram	Carbohydrate: 6 grams
Vegetable exchanges: 1	Saturated fat: 0 grams	Dietary fiber: 1 gram
Calories: 33	Cholesterol: 0 milligrams	Sugars: 4 grams
Calories from fat: 5	Sodium: 35 milligrams	Protein: 1 gram

Grilled Pacific Salmon

YIELD: 8 servings

2 pounds salmon fillet, skin on, all
    bones removed
¼ cup low-sodium soy sauce
¼ cup water
2 tablespoons balsamic vinegar

1 tablespoon finely minced onion
2 teaspoons finely minced garlic
1 teaspoon Splenda (sugar substitute)
1 lemon, cut into 8 wedges
    (optional)

Rinse the salmon fillet in cold water and pat it dry with paper towels. Run your fingers along the fillet to feel for tiny pin bones. The pin bones run from the head to about two-thirds the length of the fillet, appearing about every ½ inch. Pull out the bones using a pair of clean tweezers. Place the salmon in a nonreactive dish—glass or enamel. In a separate bowl, mix together all the other ingredients. Pour this mixture over the fish and marinate for 12 to 24 hours, turning fish 2 or 3 times.

An hour before serving, light your grill so that one side is hot and the other side is medium-hot. Lightly oil the grates on your grill just before cooking. Take the fish out of the marinade and cook it on the hot section, flesh side down, for 1 minute. Carefully rotate it a quarter turn and cook for another minute. Flip fish over and continue to cook for 8 to 10 minutes on the medium-hot section, rotating a quarter turn if necessary to get even cooking. Do not overcook. Salmon should be opaque and flaky. Transfer to a large platter and serve immediately. Garnish with lemon if desired.

Serving size: 3 ounces	Total fat: 15 grams	Carbohydrate: 0 grams
Medium-fat-meat ex- changes: 3	Saturated fat: 4 grams	Dietary fiber: 0 grams
	Cholesterol: 74 milli-	Sugars: 0 grams
Calories: 247	grams	Protein: 26 grams
Calories from fat: 135	Sodium: 91 milligrams	

Mango and Bourbon Chicken Breasts

YIELD: 8 servings

8 4-ounce skinless, boneless chicken breasts
1 cup peeled and minced ripe mango
1 tablespoon Worcestershire sauce
1 tablespoon rice wine vinegar
2 teaspoons Dijon mustard
¼ cup bourbon*

¼ cup minced red pepper
¼ cup minced onion
1 teaspoon finely chopped cilantro leaves
2–3 drops of Tabasco sauce
8 slices of mango
8 sprigs of cilantro

Wash the chicken breasts and dry them with paper towels.

Put the minced mango, Worcestershire sauce, vinegar, mustard, bourbon, pepper, onion, cilantro leaves, and Tabasco sauce into a food processor or blender and puree. Spread this marinade over the chicken breasts. Place them in a nonreactive dish, like glass, and cover. Refrigerate for at least 3 hours or up to 1 day, flipping the pieces over a few times.

*You may substitute 1 teaspoon rum extract and ¼ cup of water for the bourbon. You will save 3 calories and ½ gram of alcohol.

Prepare the grill and cook the chicken breasts over medium heat, about 10 minutes per side. Turn them frequently so they do not burn. When they're done, transfer them to a platter and garnish with a slice of mango and a sprig of cilantro atop each breast.

Serving size: 1 chicken breast	Calories from fat: 14	Carbohydrate: 4 grams
	Total fat: 2 grams	Dietary fiber: 0 grams
Very-lean-meat exchanges: 3	Saturated fat: 0 grams	Sugars: 3 grams
	Cholesterol: 66 milligrams	Protein: 26 grams
Vegetable exchanges: 1		Alcohol: 1 gram
Calories: 146	Sodium: 85 milligrams	

Russet Burgers

YIELD: 8 burgers

2 pounds lean ground beef
⅓ cup finely grated potato
¼ cup finely grated onion
1 egg

2 tablespoons sweet relish
1 teaspoon salt (optional)
1 teaspoon freshly ground black pepper

Light or turn on the grill. Heat until it is "white hot."

Mix all the ingredients well and form 8 equal-size patties. Broil them on a charcoal grill for the best flavor, but any kind of grill will suffice. Cook the burgers for 3 minutes, or until a meat thermometer inserted into the center of the burger registers 155°F or 72°C. Serve the burgers on purchased hamburger buns, if desired, with mustard and ketchup on the side.

Serving size: ⅛ recipe	Total fat: 15 grams	Sodium: 388 (89)* milligrams
Medium-fat-meat exchanges: 3	Saturated fat: 6 grams	
	Cholesterol: 98 milligrams	Carbohydrate: 3 grams
Calories: 238		Protein: 23 grams
Calories from fat: 131		

*Figure in parentheses does not include salt.

Baked Beans Canadian Style

YIELD: 12 servings

1 pound white navy beans
⅓ cup blackstrap molasses
¼ cup ketchup
½ can tomatoes, drained, diced

2 tablespoons Dijon mustard
1 small onion, finely diced
1 tablespoon Worcestershire sauce
1 teaspoon Tabasco sauce

Preheat the oven to 250°.

In the refrigerator, soak the beans overnight in 6 cups of water.

Drain the beans. In 6 cups of fresh water, bring the beans to a boil in a 3-quart Dutch oven. Then turn the heat down to medium and skim off any scum that rises to the top. Add the molasses, ketchup, canned tomatoes, mustard, onion, Worcestershire, and Tabasco. Cover and bake for 6 hours. Remove the cover and stir. Add a little water if the beans are dry. Bake for 1 more hour, uncovered, stirring a few times.

Serving size: ¾ cup	Total fat: 1 gram	Carbohydrate: 31 grams
Starch exchanges: 2	Saturated fat: 0 grams	Dietary fiber: 10 grams
Calories: 162	Cholesterol: 0 milligrams	Sugars: 7 grams
Calories from fat: 6	Sodium: 119 milligrams	Protein: 9 grams

Vegetable Kabobs

1 small, firm eggplant, peeled and cut into 6 1-inch squares, ½ inch thick
Pinch of salt
1 small onion, cut into 6 wedges
6 mushrooms, each about 1 inch round
1 small red pepper, seeds removed, cut into 1-inch squares
1 small green pepper, seeds removed, cut into 1-inch squares

1 small zucchini, cut into 6 1-inch squares, ½ inch thick
1 large Roma tomato, cut into 6 wedges
2 tablespoons olive oil
¼ teaspoon salt
¼ teaspoon freshly ground black pepper

Sprinkle the eggplant pieces with a pinch of salt, toss, and let rest for 20 minutes. Meanwhile, prepare all the other vegetables. Toss the onion, mushrooms, peppers, zucchini, and eggplant with the olive oil. If you are using wooden skewers, first soak them in water for at least 1 hour. Thread each skewer with 1 piece of each vegetable, starting with mushroom, tomato, onion, and red pepper, then adding eggplant, green pepper, and zucchini. Cover the kabobs and set them aside in the refrigerator until you're ready to grill. Cook them on a medium-hot grill about 3 to 4 minutes per side, turning them until all 4 sides are lightly browned. Season with salt and pepper to taste.

Serving size: 1 kabob	Total fat: 2 grams	Carbohydrate: 10 grams
Vegetable exchanges: 2	Saturated fat: 0 grams	Dietary fiber: 3 grams
Calories: 59	Cholesterol: 0 milligrams	Sugars: 6 grams
Calories from fat: 16	Sodium: 107 milligrams	Protein: 2 grams

Maple Walnut Brownies

YIELD: 16 brownies

½ cup (1 stick) butter
½ cup light brown sugar
½ cup sugar-free maple syrup
2 teaspoons maple-flavored extract
¾ cup plus 2 tablespoons all-purpose
  flour

¼ teaspoon baking soda
Pinch of salt
½ cup chopped walnuts

Preheat the oven to 350°.

Melt the butter over low heat. Remove it from the heat and blend with the brown sugar, maple syrup, and maple extract in a medium mixing bowl. Set aside. Sift together the flour, baking soda, and salt. Blend these dry ingredients into the butter mixture using a rubber spatula. Fold in the walnuts. Spray a 9-inch-square baking pan with cooking spray. Pour the batter into the pan and bake 25 minutes, or until a toothpick inserted into the center comes out clean.

Serving size: 1 brownie	Total fat: 8 grams	Carbohydrate: 12 grams
Starch exchanges: 1	Saturated fat: 4 grams	Dietary fiber: 0 grams
Fat exchanges: 1	Cholesterol: 16 milli-	Sugars: 4 grams
Calories: 127	grams	Protein: 1 gram
Calories from fat: 72	Sodium: 106 milligrams	

Red, White, and Blueberry Chiffon Cake

YIELD: 1 8-by-12-inch cake

2 cups all-purpose flour
1 cup plus 1 tablespoon Splenda
   (sugar substitute)
1 tablespoon baking powder
½ teaspoon salt
½ cup oil
7 eggs, separated
½ cup orange juice

¼ cup water
2 teaspoons vanilla extract
2 teaspoons grated orange zest
½ teaspoon cream of tartar
1 pint fresh strawberries
½ pint fresh blueberries
1 cup Cool Whip Lite whipped
   topping

Preheat the oven to 325°.

Sift together the flour, 1 cup of the Splenda, the baking powder, and salt in the mixing bowl of an electric mixer fitted with the paddle attachment. Make a well in center of the dry ingredients. Add the oil, egg yolks, orange juice, water, vanilla and orange zest into the well and beat until smooth.

In a separate bowl, make a meringue by whipping the egg whites, cream of tartar, and the remaining 1 tablespoon of Splenda until the egg whites form a stiff peak. Take a third of the flour mixture and gently fold it into the meringue. Then fold the meringue back into the remainder of the flour mixture. Pour the batter into a 12-by-8-inch pan that has been sprayed lightly with cooking spray. Bake for 30 to 35 minutes. The cake should be lightly browned and spring back to the touch. Allow the cake to cool 30 minutes and then remove it from the pan, placing it onto a serving tray. Cool it in refrigerator 30 more minutes before proceeding. In the meantime, wash and slice the strawberries and wash the blueberries. Dry the fruit and toss together. Spread the whipped topping evenly over the cake. Sprinkle fruit evenly over the topping. Cut into 24 pieces.

Serving size: 1 piece	Total fat: 7 grams	Carbohydrate: 12 grams
Starch exchanges: 1	Saturated fat: 1 gram	Dietary fiber: 1 gram
Fat exchanges: 1	Cholesterol: 62 milli-	Sugars: 2 grams
Calories: 122	grams	Protein: 3 grams
Calories from fat: 59	Sodium: 118 milligrams	

August

Happy Birthday

Happy Birthday

Every day is someone's birthday.

Both the day a person is born and the anniversary of that day are known as a birthday. Everyone has one, and it is a *special* day! When you are young, you anticipate the day with great longing. Little children tend to count the time between birthdays, anxious to be a year older. But as we get older, our attitudes change. Many older people celebrate their birthdays but do not acknowledge which birthday they're celebrating. Some people, like the famous comedian Jack Benny, stay thirty-nine forever. As time goes on, attitudes generally change again. When people live to the ripe old age of eight-five or ninety, they tend to boast about their age. Those who make it to a hundred or more often get special greetings from the White House and Willard Scott on the *Today* show.

If you have a child who has diabetes, you can work with his or her health-care team to figure out how you can adjust the insulin dosage to allow for special treats. If the birthday falls during a good-weather season in your area, plan a party outdoors. That way the children can run and play without worry about breaking things.

If you have an outdoor party, plan games in which all the children can participate. Hopscotch and Red Light/Green Light are old favorites enjoyed by all. Have your child help you plan the party, shop for the decorations, and select the menu. Our menu suggestions are child-friendly, and all are finger foods. Pecan Chicken Fingers and Potato Gaufrettes are young-crowd pleasers and easy to prepare. Grape Tomatoes, Baby Carrots, and Celery Sticks are vegetables most children will readily eat, but do not hesitate to add any of your own child's favorites. The Peanut Butter and Banana Cupcake Surprise takes a little more work, but the looks on the faces of the children when they discover the ice cream make it worth the effort.

If you are celebrating with adults, make the meal elegant by using your best china, crystal, and table linens. Flowers and candles always add a festive touch. The menu exemplifies how delicious healthful choices can be. Put birthday candles in the Chocolate Cream Pie—and celebrate!

Whatever you do on your birthday, just don't regret getting older. It is a glorious privilege.

Happy Birthday (Child)

Pecan Chicken Fingers

Potato Gaufrettes

Grape Tomatoes, Baby Carrots, Celery Sticks

Peanut Butter and Banana Cupcake Surprise

Pecan Chicken Fingers

YIELD: 4 servings

½ cup quick oats
¼ cup finely chopped pecans or
  walnuts
⅛ teaspoon garlic salt
⅛ teaspoon freshly ground black
  pepper

⅛ teaspoon paprika
⅛ teaspoon poultry seasoning
12 ounces skinless, boneless chicken
  breasts

Preheat the oven to 350°.

Spread the oats on a cookie sheet and bake until they are lightly browned. Remove the cookie sheet from the oven, and increase the temperature to 425°. Mix the toasted oats and the nuts with the seasonings. Flatten the chicken to about ½ inch thick with a mallet. Cut the chicken into strips about 1 inch wide and 3 inches long. Coat the chicken on all sides with the oat/nut mixture. Lay the chicken pieces flat on a baking pan coated with cooking spray and bake for about 12 minutes. The chicken will be opaque inside, and the breading will be a rich brown color.

Serving size: ¼ of recipe	Calories from fat: 49	Sodium: 75 milligrams
Starch exchanges: ½	Total fat: 5 grams	Carbohydrate: 8 grams
Very-lean-meat	Saturated fat: 1gram	Dietary fiber: 1 gram
exchanges: 3	Cholesterol: 49 milli-	Sugars: 0 grams
Calories: 177	grams	Protein: 22 grams

Potato Gaufrettes

YIELD: 4 servings

2 baking potatoes
2 teaspoons vegetable oil
½ teaspoon freshly ground black
    pepper
¼ teaspoon onion salt

¼ teaspoon garlic salt
¼ teaspoon paprika
⅛ teaspoon ground thyme
⅛ teaspoon ground rosemary

Preheat the oven to 450°.

Wash the potatoes well and cut them into slices ¼ inch thick with a crinkle/wavy knife if you have one. Put the rest of the ingredients into a plastic bag and shake well. Add the potatoes and shake well to coat. Coat a baking pan with cooking spray and arrange the seasoned potatoes on it in a single layer. Bake them for 15 minutes. Turn the potatoes over and bake them for 10 minutes longer, or until crisp.

Serving size: ¼ recipe	Total fat: 2 grams	Carbohydrate: 17 grams
Starch exchanges: 1	Saturated fat: 0 grams	Dietary fiber: 0 grams
Calories: 99	Cholesterol: 0 milligrams	Sugars: 0 grams
Calories from fat: 22	Sodium: 101 milligrams	Protein: 3 grams

Grape Tomatoes, Baby Carrots, and Celery Sticks

These vegetables are popular choices with most children. And there's no recipe necessary here! Simply arrange them attractively on a platter and let the little ones help themselves. Feel free to add or substitute any vegetable your child likes. There are many varieties of miniature vegetables available these days, and they are a good way to introduce your child to new vegetables.

Peanut Butter and Banana Cupcake Surprise (filled with chocolate ice cream)

YIELD: 1½ dozen 2¾-inch cupcakes

Cupcakes

2 medium bananas, very ripe
2¾ cups cake flour
¾ cup Splenda (sugar substitute)
½ cup brown sugar
1 teaspoon salt
½ cup shortening

2 eggs
2 egg yolks
1 tablespoon baking soda
1 tablespoon baking powder
¾ cup 2% milk
2 teaspoons vanilla extract

Preheat the oven to 350°.

Mix together the bananas, ¾ cup of the cake flour, the Splenda, brown sugar, salt, and shortening in the bowl of an electric mixer on medium speed for 4 minutes. Scrape down the sides of the bowl twice during mixing. Add the eggs and yolks gradually while continuing to mix on medium speed. Scrape down sides of bowl once more.

Sift together the remaining 2 cups of cake flour, the baking soda and baking powder and add to the above mixture. Blend slightly and then begin to add the milk and vanilla gradually until they're incorporated. Scrape down the sides of bowl and mix until smooth. Pour the batter into cupcake pans that are either coated with cooking spray or lined with paper cupcake cups. Bake for approximately 18 to 20 minutes. Test for doneness by inserting a toothpick into the center of a cupcake. It should come out clean. Remove the cupcakes from the pans and cool them completely before icing.

Icing

½ cup peanut butter
3 cups Cool Whip Lite whipped topping
2¼ cups sugar-free chocolate ice cream

Rainbow sprinkles
Chocolate syrup

Place the peanut butter in a bowl and beat it by hand with a rubber spatula. Add 1 cup of the whipped topping and beat until smooth. Add the remaining topping and fold in until smooth. Ice the tops of the cupcakes and add sprinkles.

To serve, slice off the top third of each cupcake and set these pieces aside. Use a tablespoon to scoop out a cavity in the bottom piece of each cupcake. Fill the hollow with ice cream. Replace the reserved tops. Drizzle some chocolate syrup on each plate and place cupcake on plate. Sprinkle some rainbow sprinkles around the plate. Serve immediately.

Serving size: 1 cupcake	Calories from fat: 92	Sodium: 384 milligrams*
Starch exchanges: 1	Total fat: 10 grams	Carbohydrate: 30 grams
Fruit exchanges: 1	Saturated fat: 3 grams	Dietary fiber: 1 gram
Fat exchanges: 2	Cholesterol: 39 milli-	Sugars: 11 grams
Calories: 228	grams	Protein: 6 grams

*This recipe is not recommended for low-sodium diets.

Happy Birthday (Adult)

Iced Basil Gazpacho

Veal Marengo

Noodles

Rosemary Zucchini and Yellow Squash

Chocolate Cream Pie

Iced Basil Gazpacho

YIELD: 6 servings

2 medium ripe tomatoes, cored and seeded, diced into ¼-inch pieces

2 large cucumbers, peeled, seeded, and diced into ¼-inch pieces

1 medium green pepper, diced into ¼-inch pieces

1 small onion, peeled, and finely diced

2 teaspoons olive oil

1 clove garlic, very finely minced

1 tablespoon chopped fresh parsley

1 cup water

11½-ounce can V-8 juice

2 tablespoons red wine vinegar

Dash of freshly ground black pepper

½ tablespoon chopped fresh basil

Combine all the ingredients except the basil. Refrigerate, covered, for at least 2 hours but not more than 24 hours. Before serving, add the fresh basil and ladle into chilled bowls.

Serving size: 4 ounces	Total fat: 2 grams	Carbohydrate: 9 grams
Vegetable exchanges: 2	Saturated fat: 0 grams	Dietary fiber: 2 grams
Calories: 56	Cholesterol: 0 milligrams	Sugars: 4 grams
Calories from fat: 16	Sodium: 156 milligrams	Protein: 1 gram

Veal Marengo

YIELD: 4 servings

1½ pounds veal leg or loin,* flattened to ¹⁄₁₆ inch thick
Flour to dust veal
1 tablespoon olive oil
2 tablespoons minced raw onion
1 teaspoon minced garlic clove
8 ounces mushrooms, sliced
1½ tablespoons tomato paste
2 tablespoons white wine

16 small pearl onions, frozen
4 ripe olives, sliced
1 teaspoon tarragon
½ teaspoon white pepper
Egg noodles (prepared according to package directions)
Fresh rosemary sprigs (optional, for garnish)

Lightly dust the veal with flour. Heat a pan on high, and then add the olive oil. When the oil is hot, quickly sear the veal on both sides for about 1 minute, or until lightly browned. Remove the veal to a platter. In the same pan, add the onion, garlic, and mushrooms and sauté over medium heat for 5 minutes. Add the tomato paste and stir well. Add the wine, pearl onions, and olives and continue to cook for another 2 minutes. Add the tarragon and pepper. Stir. Return the veal to the pan just long enough to heat it through. Place the veal slices on a bed of prepared noodles arranged artistically on a plate and spoon the sauce from the pan over all. Garnish the plate with a sprig of fresh rosemary if desired.

Serving size: ¼ recipe	Calories from fat: 71	Carbohydrate: 6 grams
Very-lean-meat exchanges: 5	Total fat: 8 grams	Dietary fiber: 1 gram
Vegetable exchanges: 1	Saturated fat: 2 grams	Sugars: 1 gram
Fat exchanges: 1	Cholesterol: 133 milligrams	Protein: 39 grams
Calories: 255	Sodium: 159 milligrams	

* This recipe easily adapts to chicken by using skinless, boneless breasts flattened thin. The chicken will take just a little longer to cook.

Rosemary Zucchini and Yellow Squash

YIELD: 4 servings

1 small zucchini
1 small yellow squash
½ tablespoon olive oil
3 sprigs of fresh rosemary *or*
    ½ teaspoon dried rosemary

⅛ teaspoon salt
⅛ teaspoon white pepper

Cut the zucchini and squash on the bias about ½ inch thick, making about 8 pieces from each. If you are using fresh rosemary, coat the vegetables with the olive oil and add the rosemary. If you are using dried rosemary, mix the olive oil and dried rosemary and then coat the vegetables with this mixture. Set aside for 30 minutes or longer. Prepare the grill so that it is hot. Carefully place the vegetables on the grill and grill for 2 to 3 minutes on each side, until they are tender. If you prefer, you may use the broiler in your oven. Broil just long enough to make the vegetables tender and not mushy. Sprinkle with a little salt and white pepper if desired.

Serving size: ¼ recipe	Total fat: 1 gram	Carbohydrate: 3 grams
Vegetable exchanges: 1	Saturated fat: 0 grams	Dietary fiber: 0 grams
Calories: 17	Cholesterol: 0 milligrams	Sugars: 1 gram
Calories from fat: 5	Sodium: 77 milligrams	Protein: 1 gram

Chocolate Cream Pie

YIELD: 1 9-inch deep-dish pie

1 9-inch deep-dish pie shell, pre-baked until golden brown and cooled (available frozen)

2½ cups 2% milk

2 ounces unsweetened chocolate

2 ounces semisweet chocolate

1 tablespoon plus 2 teaspoons Equal (16 packets)

Pinch of salt

2 tablespoons cornstarch

3 tablespoons unsweetened cocoa powder

2 eggs

1 tablespoon butter, chopped

1 teaspoon vanilla extract

1 cup Cool Whip Lite whipped topping (optional)

Boil 2¼ cups of the milk in a heavy saucepan. Chop both chocolates very fine. Remove the milk from the heat and stir in the chocolates. Stir until completely melted. Sift together the Equal, salt, cornstarch, and cocoa. Add the remaining ¼ cup milk to the dry ingredients and beat until smooth. Beat in the eggs. Using a wire whisk, gradually whisk in ½ cup of the hot chocolate milk to the egg mixture. Return the saucepan of chocolate milk to medium heat. Gradually add the egg mixture while whisking. Reduce the heat to low and cook for 2 minutes, stirring constantly. The mixture will thicken. Remove it from the heat and stir in the chopped butter and vanilla. Pour the mixture into the prepared pie shell. Cover it with plastic wrap and chill in the refrigerator. Allow the filling to set for at least 3 hours. If you wish, top each piece with whipped topping upon serving.

Serving size: ⅒ of pie	Total fat: 13 grams	Carbohydrate: 18 grams
Starch exchanges: 1	Saturated fat: 6 grams	Dietary fiber: 2 grams
Fat exchanges: 2½	Cholesterol: 51 milli-grams	Sugars: 5 grams
Calories: 195		Protein: 5 grams
Calories from fat: 114	Sodium: 153 milligrams	

September

Labor Day
Rosh Hashanah

Labor Day

First Monday in September

In June 1894, Congress passed an act making the first Monday in September a legal holiday, and each year since then Americans have celebrated this holiday, midway between the Fourth of July and Thanksgiving. While we know it as the final long weekend of summer, its origins lie in the industrial revolution.

Factories, nonexistent prior to 1750, became widespread by 1850. Safety standards and regulations were unheard of, and factories were dangerous and inhumane workplaces. Employers were concerned about profits, not the safety of the workers, and people worked long hours for little pay.

The labor movement began in the late 1800s because workers, wanting to improve their lot, joined together to form unions. In the early days protests were not peaceful, and violence and bloodshed were part of any labor strike. About this time union workers began taking unpaid time off to hold parades and picnics and listen to speeches on how to right the wrongs of industrialized society.

Thus the holiday was born. It became official shortly after the end of the infamous and bloody Pullman strike of 1894. As it was an election year, President Cleveland wanted to appease the workingman so he signed the legislation making Labor Day official. Although he gave birth to this holiday, Cleveland was not reelected. Yet to this day the unions continue to support political candidates who share their ideology.

Union membership has declined over the years, with only about 15 percent of Americans belonging to unions. Nevertheless, all of us, whether we belong to a union or not, have benefited from the struggles of the early union members. Things that employees now take for granted—the forty-hour workweek, paid vacations, health insurance—are the result of their fight.

So in the tradition of the day, enjoy a break from work, have a picnic, include some physical activity, and remember those pioneers who made all this possible. Our menu is best for a party. If you plan on having a large group, you can now serve a variety of foods, and your guests who have special health needs can select those foods that fit their need and desires.

Slice the turkey and tri-tip steaks so that your guests can have some of each without going overboard. All the salads feature dressings that are low in fat and high in flavor. And the Peach and Blueberry Cobbler lends itself to an alternative sweetener, which automatically lowers the sugar and calorie content, enabling all to enjoy this treat.

Labor Day

Vegetable Salad with Balsamic Vinaigrette

All-American Pasta Salad

Three-Bean Salad

Red, White, and Blue Potato Salad

Citrus-Marinated Turkey Steaks

Tri-tip Beer Steak

Peach and Blueberry Cobbler

or

Sun-Dried Cherry and Pineapple Bar

Vegetable Salad with Balsamic Vinaigrette

YIELD: 8 servings

3 medium vine-ripened tomatoes
1 cucumber, English or seedless
1 medium onion, sliced
2 teaspoons fresh thyme, chopped

Freshly ground black pepper
½ cup Balsamic Vinaigrette (see recipe, p. 121)
Fresh basil leaves for garnish

Remove the stems from the tomatoes and cut the tomatoes into small wedges. Set aside. Wash the cucumber and with the tines of a fork cut little grooves about ¼ inch deep into the sides by dragging the fork down lengthwise. Repeat all the way around. Cut the cucumber in half lengthwise and slice it across about ¼ inch thick. (If you use a regular cucumber, be sure to remove seeds by dragging a spoon down the inside of each half.) Place the cucumber slices in a large bowl. Add the sliced onion. Mix in the thyme, pepper, and vinaigrette. Toss well. Add in the tomatoes and gently mix. Place in a serving bowl and garnish with fresh basil.

Serving size: ⅛ recipe, about ¾ cup	Total fat: 0 grams	Dietary fiber: 1 gram
	Saturated fat: 0 grams	Sugars: 5 grams
Vegetable exchanges: 1	Cholesterol: 0 milligrams	Protein: 1 gram
Calories: 31	Sodium: 32 milligrams	
Calories from fat: 3	Carbohydrate: 7 grams	

All-American Pasta Salad

YIELD: 8 servings

8 ounces ditalini pasta or other small pasta
1 cup plain yogurt
1 tablespoon lemon juice
2 teaspoons curry powder
1 tablespoon finely chopped parsley
1 teaspoon white pepper
2 teaspoons finely chopped fresh basil

1 medium cucumber, peeled, seeded, and diced into ¼-inch pieces
½ small onion, finely diced
1 small green pepper, seeded and diced into ¼-inch pieces
1 small tomato, cut in half, seeded, and diced into ¼-inch pieces

Cook the pasta per package directions. While the pasta is cooking, mix together the yogurt, lemon juice, curry powder, parsley, white pepper, and basil in a large bowl. Add the cucumber, onion, green bell pepper, and tomato. Blend well. When the pasta is cooked, cool it under cold running water. Drain the pasta well and add it to the bowl. Toss, cover, and refrigerate until ready to serve.

Serving size: ⅛ recipe, approximately ¾ cup	Calories from fat: 10	Carbohydrate: 27 grams
Starch exchanges: 1	Total fat: 1 gram	Dietary fiber: 2 grams
Vegetable exchanges: 2	Saturated fat: 0 grams	Sugars: 4 grams
Calories: 141	Cholesterol: 1 milligram	Protein: 6 grams
	Sodium: 25 milligrams	

Three-Bean Salad

YIELD: 8 servings

1 15-ounce can red kidney beans, 50% less salt
1 15-ounce can white navy beans, 50% less salt
1 15-ounce can black beans, 50% less salt
12 cups water
½ medium white onion, cut into short strips
½ medium red pepper, diced into small pieces

½ medium green pepper, diced into small pieces
2 teaspoons Dijon mustard
1 tablespoon white wine vinegar
½ cup plain nonfat yogurt
8 drops Tabasco sauce
1 tablespoon finely chopped fresh parsley

Drain all the beans in a colander and then soak them in 6 cups of cold water for 15 minutes. Drain well. Bring 6 fresh cups of water to a boil on high heat in a large pot. Add the beans. When the water returns to a boil, turn off heat and drain the beans. After they are well drained, place them in a large bowl. Add the onion and peppers and mix gently. In a separate bowl, mix the mustard, vinegar, yogurt, and Tabasco sauce. Add this dressing to the beans and mix well. Sprinkle with chopped parsley and refrigerate until ready to serve. Serve chilled.

Serving size: ⅛ recipe, approximately ¾ cup	Total fat: 1 gram	Dietary fiber: 9 grams
	Saturated fat: 0 grams	Sugars: 3 grams
Starch exchanges: 2	Cholesterol: 1 milligram	Protein: 10 grams
Calories: 153	Sodium: 224 milligrams	
Calories from fat: 6	Carbohydrate: 29 grams	

Red, White, and Blue Potato Salad

YIELD: 8 servings

½ pound Peruvian Blue potatoes,* washed well and cut into ¾-inch cubes

½ pound Red Bliss potatoes, washed well and cut into ¾-inch cubes

½ pound round white potatoes, washed well and cut into ¾-inch cubes

Freshly ground black pepper

4 strips of turkey bacon, cut into ¼-inch strips

¼ cup red onion, cut into thin strips

¼ cup white wine vinegar

¼ cup Chicken Stock (see recipe, p. 21)

2 green onions, cut small

Cook all the potatoes, covered, in lightly salted water for 15 to 20 minutes, until tender. Drain. Add the pepper to taste and set aside in a large bowl. Sauté the bacon until it is light brown. Add the red onion and cook for 2 more minutes. Add the vinegar and stock. Bring to a boil. Cool for 2 minutes and then pour this liquid over the potatoes. Mix well but gently,

* If Peruvian Blue potatoes are not available, increase the amount of either or both of the other potatoes.

being careful not to break up the potatoes. Sprinkle the green onions on top and serve chilled.

Serving size: ⅛ recipe, approximately ½ cup	Total fat: 1 gram	Dietary fiber: 2 grams
Starch exchanges: 1	Saturated fat: 0 grams	Sugars: 2 grams
Calories: 95	Cholesterol: 5 milligrams	Protein: 3 grams
Calories from fat: 13	Sodium: 133 milligrams	
	Carbohydrate: 18 grams	

Citrus-Marinated Turkey Steaks

YIELD: 6 servings

Turkey

1½ pounds turkey cutlets, about ⅜ inch thick, cut from the breast

Marinade

2 tablespoons lemon juice
2 tablespoons lime juice
2 tablespoons Worcestershire sauce
¼ cup dry white wine
2 teaspoons fresh rosemary leaves
2 teaspoons fresh thyme leaves

2 teaspoons finely chopped fresh parsley
2 tablespoons olive oil
1 teaspoon freshly ground black pepper

Garnish

2 teaspoons rosemary
2 teaspoons thyme

2 teaspoons parsley

Rinse the turkey cutlets and pat them dry with paper towels. Mix together all the marinade ingredients in a separate bowl. Pour a fourth of the marinade into a glass dish just large enough to hold the turkey steaks flat. Lay in the turkey. Pour the balance of the marinade over the turkey. Cover and refrigerate 1 to 4 hours.

When the grill is medium-hot, grill the turkey cutlets on an oiled grate for 6 minutes on each side, or until no longer pink in the middle. When the cutlets are done, cut them into 6 portions. Arrange the turkey on a platter and sprinkle it with the herb garnish.

Serving size: 4 ounces	Total fat: 2 grams	Carbohydrate: 0 grams
Very-lean-meat	Saturated fat: 0 grams	Dietary fiber: 0 grams
exchanges: 4	Cholesterol: 70 milli-	Sugars: 0 grams
Calories: 140	grams	Protein: 28 grams
Calories from fat: 20	Sodium: 65 milligrams	

Tri-tip Beer Steak

YIELD: 6 servings

1–1½ pounds tri-tip steak, ¾ inch thick
1 12-ounce bottle of beer
¼ cup low-sodium soy sauce
¼ cup water
4 cloves garlic, finely minced

2 tablespoons Dijon mustard
2 green onions, thinly sliced
2 tablespoons ketchup
1 teaspoon freshly ground black pepper

Place the steak in a plastic zipper bag or in a glass dish. Pour the beer into a small saucepan and bring to a boil. Reduce the heat and simmer until it has reduced to ½ cup. Add the remainder of the ingredients and mix well. Pour this over the steak. Seal the bag or cover the dish and refrigerate for 12 to 24 hours, turning occasionally.

Light grill, and when it is medium-hot, remove the steak from the marinade and grill for 10 to 12 minutes, turning once. Brush with marinade a few times while cooking. When it is grilled to your liking, slice the meat diagonally across the grain in ½-inch-wide strips.

Serving size: 3 ounces	Total fat: 2 grams	Carbohydrate: 0 grams
Very-lean-meat	Saturated fat: 1 gram	Dietary fiber: 0 grams
exchanges: 3	Cholesterol: 43 milli-	Sugars: 0 grams
Calories: 122	grams	Protein: 23 grams
Calories from fat: 19	Sodium: 177 milligrams	

Peach and Blueberry Cobbler

YIELD: 6 individual servings (use 6-ounce ovenproof dishes)

Pie Dough

1 cup plus 3 tablespoons all-purpose
   flour
1 teaspoon Equal (3 packets)
¼ cup butter, chopped, at room temperature

1 egg
¼ cup cold 2% milk

Mix the flour and Equal in the bowl of an electric mixer fitted with the paddle attachment. Distribute the chopped butter over the top of the flour. Mix it in, on low speed, until small lumps form. Add the egg and milk, and mix just to combine and form a dough. Remove the dough from the bowl and shape it into an oval. Wrap this in plastic and refrigerate it at least a half hour before use.

Remove the dough from the refrigerator and cut it in half. Cover one half tightly with plastic wrap and refrigerate it for future use. Roll the remaining dough out on a lightly floured surface. Use an appropriate size round cookie cutter to cut it into 6 circles ½ inch wider than the ovenproof dishes. Cut a ¼-inch hole in the middle of each circle.

Peach and Blueberry Filling

3 cups frozen sliced peaches, thawed
½ teaspoon cinnamon
2 teaspoons Equal (7 packets)
¼ teaspoon nutmeg

1 tablespoon minute tapioca
½ cup fresh blueberries
1 egg

Preheat the oven to 400°.

Place the thawed peach slices in mixing bowl. In a separate bowl, combine the cinnamon, Equal, nutmeg, and tapioca. Sprinkle the cinnamon mixture over peaches and fold in with rubber spatula to combine completely. Fold in the blueberries; distribute this mixture evenly among the ovenproof dishes. Break the egg into a small bowl and beat thoroughly. Using a pastry brush, lightly wash the edges of the dishes with beaten egg. Place pie-dough circles on top and brush them with beaten egg. Place the dishes on cookie sheet and bake for approximately 15 to 20 minutes, until tops are golden brown. Remove them from oven and let them set 10 minutes to cool slightly before serving.

Serving size: 1 cobbler	Total fat: 5 grams	Carbohydrate: 33 grams
Starch exchanges: 2	Saturated fat: 3 grams	Dietary fiber: 4 grams
Fat exchanges: ½	Cholesterol: 29 milli-	Sugars: 16 grams
Calories: 182	grams	Protein: 3 grams
Calories from fat: 44	Sodium: 149 milligrams	

Sun-Dried Cherry and Pineapple Bar

YIELD: 20 servings

1 cup sun-dried cherries
2 cups hot water
16 ounces crushed pineapple, not drained
2 teaspoons cornstarch
2 teaspoons Equal (7 packets)
1 cup oats

½ cup chopped walnuts
1 cup all-purpose flour
½ teaspoon cinnamon
2 egg whites (reserve yolks for another use)
¼ cup canola oil

Preheat the oven to 375°.

Soak the cherries in 2 cups of hot water for 5 minutes, then drain. Place the pineapple and cherries in a saucepan and sprinkle the cornstarch over them. Place the pot on medium heat and cook for approximately 5 minutes, stirring constantly. The liquid will thicken. Remove from the heat and stir in 1 teaspoon of the Equal. Set aside to cool.

Combine the oats, walnuts, flour, cinnamon, and the remaining 1 teaspoon Equal in the bowl of an electric mixer fitted with the paddle attachment. Mix to combine. Add the egg whites and blend in; the mixture will resemble coarse meal. Add the oil and blend in. Take two-thirds of the oat mixture and press it tightly and evenly into an 8-inch square pan that has been coated with cooking spray. Next, spread the pineapple-cherry mixture over the bottom layer of oat mixture. Press it down and spread it out evenly. Sprinkle on the remaining oat crumbs and bake for 20 to 25 minutes, until the top is golden brown. Cool before cutting. Cut into 20 equal-size bars.

Serving size: 1 bar	Total fat: 5 grams	Dietary fiber: 1 gram
Starch exchanges: 1	Saturated fat: 1 gram	Sugars: 8 grams
Fat exchanges: 1	Cholesterol: 0 milligrams	Protein: 2 grams
Calories: 122	Sodium: 7 milligrams	
Calories from fat: 42	Carbohydrate: 19 grams	

Rosh Hashanah

Rosh Hashanah, or Jewish New Year, is celebrated on the first and second day of the month of Tishri, the first lunar month, usually in September.

R osh Hashanah is a very important holiday in Judaism. It is generally celebrated for two days, considered one long forty-eight-hour day. This special time has many meanings.

It commemorates the creation of the world as well as the Day of Judgment. It is also a day of remembrance, a time to look back at the history of Judaism, and a special time of prayer for Israel. And it is Jewish New Year, complete with greeting cards and special foods. On Rosh Hashanah the shofar (ram's horn) is blown to announce the beginning of the High Holy Days.

When leaving the synagogue after Rosh Hashanah services, celebrants say to one another, "May you be inscribed in the Book of Life." This greeting comes from the tradition that tells us that on this day God opens three books. He records the names of the righteous in the Book of Life, the names of the wicked who will be punished by death in the second book, and the names of those who have not yet been judged in the third book. Those in the third book have ten days to repent and atone for their transgressions. The High Holy Days end ten days after Rosh Hashanah on Yom Kippur, the Day of Atonement, which is a day of prayer and fasting.

Families gather together to observe the holiday of Rosh Hashanah, with the festivities beginning at sundown, when a special meal is served. Traditional menu items are apples dipped in honey; challah, the traditional egg bread; and carrots. The challah is not braided, as it is the rest of the year, but baked in a circle or crown shape. The circle symbolizes the cycle of life and the wish that the next year will go smoothly. It is also shaped like a crown to remind everyone that God is king of the universe. The challah is dipped in honey before it is eaten, as sweets eaten at this meal bring hope for a sweet year ahead, one filled with blessings and abundance.

Carrots, a naturally sweet food, are a featured dish on many holiday tables. Our Carrot and Pineapple Tzimmes (sweet stew) is delicious, low in fat, a great source of beta-carotene, and it makes a perfect accompaniment to the Lemon-Roasted Chicken entrée. In Yiddish making a *tzimmes* means making a big fuss about something—yet another reason that this is an appropriate dish for this special day!

All the sweets served at this meal may *appear* to present a dilemma to the person with diabetes. But if you are counting your carbohydrates, you can adjust your portion sizes and/or your medication to allow you to participate in the festivities. Use the nutrition information provided with each recipe to make appropriate choices. And check with your health-care team if you have questions.

Rosh Hashanah

Old-Fashioned Cabbage Soup

Lemon-Roasted Chicken

Lentils and Rice with Caramelized Onions

Carrot and Pineapple Tzimmes

Challah

Carrot Cake with Vanilla-Pineapple Icing

Old-Fashioned Cabbage Soup

YIELD: 12 servings

1 tablespoon olive oil
1 medium onion, minced
8 ounces mushrooms, diced small
2 medium carrots, minced
4 cups green cabbage, quartered,
   core removed, and thinly sliced
1 bay leaf

6 cups Chicken Stock (see recipe,
   p. 21)
2 medium potatoes, peeled and
   cubed small
15-ounce can no-salt-added tomatoes, chopped, not drained

Heat the olive oil in a 4-quart pot over medium heat and sauté the onion for about 2 minutes. Add the mushrooms and carrots and cook for 2 more minutes. Add the cabbage, bay leaf, and stock. Bring to a boil, turn the heat down to low when the soup boils, and simmer for 20 minutes. Add the potatoes and tomatoes and continue to cook for 15 minutes, or until the potatoes are tender. Remove the bay leaf. Season with salt and pepper to taste.

Serving size: 5 ounces	Total fat: 2 grams	Dietary fiber: 2 grams
Vegetable exchanges: 2	Saturated fat: 0 grams	Sugars: 4 grams
Fat exchanges: ½	Cholesterol: 0 milligrams	Protein: 3 grams
Calories: 72	Sodium: 277 milligrams	
Calories from fat: 21	Carbohydrate: 12 grams	

Lemon-Roasted Chicken

YIELD: 8 servings

4-pound whole chicken
½ cup fresh lemon juice
1 tablespoon Dijon mustard
3 cloves garlic, crushed
½ cup Chicken Stock, low sodium,
    defatted (see recipe, p. 21)

1 teaspoon lemon pepper
½ teaspoon salt
½ teaspoon paprika

Rinse the chicken under cold water, inside and out, and pat it dry with a paper towel. Place the chicken in a large plastic zipper bag. Mix together the lemon juice, mustard, garlic, and stock and pour into the bag with the chicken. Seal the bag and let the chicken marinate for 1 to 2 hours in the refrigerator, turning it every 30 minutes.

Preheat the oven to 375°.

Mix together the lemon pepper, salt, and paprika. Take the chicken out of bag and drain any marinade from the cavity. Season the chicken, both inside and out, with the seasoning mixture. Place the chicken in a roasting pan, inserting a meat thermometer into the thickest part of the breast near the wing, and cook it for 60 minutes. The thermometer should reach a minimum of 165°. Let the chicken rest for 15 minutes before cutting. Remove the skin before serving.

Serving size: 3 ounces	Total fat: 6 grams	Carbohydrate: 0 grams
Very-lean-meat	Saturated fat: 2 grams	Dietary fiber: 0 grams
exchanges: 4	Cholesterol: 76 milli-	Sugars: 0 grams
Calories: 162	grams	Protein: 25 grams
Calories from fat: 57	Sodium: 219 milligrams	

Lentils and Rice with Caramelized Onions

YIELD: 8 servings

Lentils and Rice

⅔ cup lentils
½ cup brown rice
5½ cups Chicken Stock *or* Vegetable Stock, divided (see recipes, pp. 21 and 11)
½ bay leaf

¼ cup diced celery
¼ cup diced carrots
1 clove garlic, minced
1 teaspoon olive oil
1 tablespoon chopped fresh parsley

The lentils and rice can be cooked ahead of time. Cook the dry lentils (⅔ cup will yield 1½ cups when cooked) in 3 cups of the stock for about 45 minutes. When the lentils are tender, remove them from the heat and let cool. Bring the brown rice (½ cup will yield 1½ cups rice when cooked) to a boil with 2 cups of the stock and ½ bay leaf, then reduce to a simmer and cook, covered, for 50 minutes. Remove the bay leaf and let the rice cool.

Sauté the celery, carrots, and garlic in the olive oil for 2 to 3 minutes. Add the lentils and rice and stir. Pour in the remainder of the stock, stir, cover, and simmer for 5 minutes. Turn off the heat, add the parsley, and stir. Keep the pot covered while you prepare the onions.

Caramelized Onions

2 medium onions, cut into quarters, then sliced into short strips
2 tablespoons balsamic vinegar

2 tablespoons dry red wine
1 teaspoon Splenda (sugar substitute)

Place the onion strips in a nonstick fry pan. Cook them on high heat for 5 minutes, stirring often. Turn the heat down to medium, add the vinegar, wine, and Splenda, and continue to cook, slowly, for approximately 15 minutes. The juices will start to come out of the onions and begin to caramelize. When the onions are dark brown and most of the juices are gone, they are done.

To serve, divide the lentil-rice mixture onto serving plates and top with 2 tablespoons of caramelized onions.

Serving size: ½ cup	Total fat: 1 gram	Dietary fiber: 4 grams
Starch exchanges: 1	Saturated fat: 0 grams	Sugars: 4 grams
Vegetable exchanges: 1	Cholesterol: 0 milligrams	Protein: 5 grams
Calories: 115	Sodium: 100 milligrams	
Calories from fat: 10	Carbohydrate: 21 grams	

Carrot and Pineapple Tzimmes

YIELD: 8 servings

2 large carrots, peeled and diced into large pieces
2 medium sweet potatoes, peeled and diced into large pieces
1½ cups water
½ teaspoon salt

2 tablespoons honey
½ cup pitted prunes
½ cup crushed unsweetened pineapple, drained
1 tablespoon lemon juice
1 teaspoon finely grated lemon zest

Bring the carrots, sweet potatoes, water, and salt to a boil over medium heat. Cover and cook for 15 minutes. Add the prunes, honey, lemon juice, and lemon zest. Cover and continue to simmer gently over low heat for 20 minutes or until the liquid is almost absorbed.

Serving size: ⅛ of recipe	Total fat: 0 grams	Dietary fiber: 2 grams
Vegetable exchanges: 1	Saturated fat: 0 grams	Sugars: 12 grams
Fruit exchanges: 1	Cholesterol: 0 milligrams	Protein: 1 gram
Calories: 92	Sodium: 157 milligrams	
Calories from fat: 2	Carbohydrate: 23 grams	

Challah

YIELD: 1 10-inch crown

2½ cups all-purpose flour
1 tablespoon sugar
½ teaspoon salt
½ packet active yeast
3 tablespoons margarine, softened

2 eggs
½ cup warm water
1 egg yolk
1 tablespoon cold water

Preheat the oven to 400.°

Mix ½ cup of the flour, the sugar, salt, and yeast in the bowl of an electric mixer fitted with the paddle attachment. Add the margarine and beat 2 minutes. Add the eggs and another ½ cup flour; beat 2 minutes on medium speed. Add the warm water and mix in. Add the remaining 1½ cups flour and mix in to form a soft dough. Turn the dough out onto a lightly floured surface and knead 4 to 5 minutes, until the dough is smooth. Place the dough in a lightly oiled bowl and lightly oil the top of the dough. Cover with plastic wrap. Let the dough rise in a warm place until double in size, about 50 minutes.

Remove the plastic wrap, punch down the dough, turn it out onto a lightly floured surface, and form it into a cylinder 16 inches long. Then coil the cylinder into a circle or "crown" shape. Place it on a cookie sheet sprayed with cooking spray. Beat the remaining egg yolk with the cold water to make an egg wash and use this to secure the ends of the dough together. Reserve the rest of the egg wash. Place the cookie sheet in a large plastic bag and let the dough rise in a warm place until double in size, about 45 minutes. Remove the cookie sheet from the plastic bag, gently brush the loaf with egg wash, and bake it in the preheated oven for 20 to 25 minutes.

Serving size: 1⁄16 of loaf	Total fat: 3 grams	Carbohydrate: 16 grams
Starch exchanges: 1	Saturated fat: 1 gram	Dietary fiber: 1 gram
Fat exchanges: ½	Cholesterol: 40 milli-	Sugars: 1 gram
Calories: 107	grams	Protein: 3 grams
Calories from fat: 29	Sodium: 109 milligrams	

Carrot Cake with Vanilla-Pineapple Icing

YIELD: 24 servings

Carrot Cake

½ cup butter, at room temperature
3 eggs
1 cup unsweetened pineapple juice
2 teaspoons vanilla extract
2½ cups all-purpose flour
2 teaspoons baking powder
1 teaspoon baking soda
½ teaspoon nutmeg

1 teaspoon cinnamon
Pinch of salt
3 tablespoons Equal (30 packets)
½ cup crushed unsweetened pineapple, drained
3 cups shredded carrots
½ cup coarsely chopped walnuts (optional)

Preheat the oven to 350°.

Beat soft butter in the bowl of an electric mixer until it is light and creamy. Beat in the eggs one at a time, scraping down the sides of the bowl after each addition. Beat in the pineapple juice and vanilla, scraping down again. Sift together the all-purpose flour, baking powder, baking soda, nutmeg, cinnamon, salt, and Equal. Add half the dry ingredients to the batter and mix until combined. Scrape down the bowl, add the remaining dry ingredients, and mix only until all the dry ingredients are incorporated into the batter. Add the pineapple, carrots, and walnuts if using. Mix in, scrape down, and blend until completely combined. Do not overmix. Spray an 8-by-12-inch baking pan with cooking spray. Pour the batter into the prepared pan, spread it out evenly with spatula, and bake for 30 to 35 minutes, or until a toothpick inserted in the center comes out clean. Cool and ice.

Vanilla-Pineapple Icing

8 ounces cream cheese
½ teaspoon Equal (1½ packets)
½ teaspoon vanilla extract

8 ounces crushed unsweetened
  pineapple, drained
¼ cup chopped walnuts (optional)

Beat the cream cheese and Equal in the bowl of an electric mixer until soft and creamy. Add the vanilla and pineapple, scrape down the sides of the bowl, and mix until smooth. Spread the icing over the cooled cake. Sprinkle with chopped walnuts if desired.

Serving size: 1 piece, ¹⁄₂₄ of recipe	Total fat: 10 (9)* grams	Sugars: 5 grams
Starch exchanges: 1	Saturated fat: 5 grams	Protein: 4 grams
Fat exchanges: 2	Cholesterol: 47 milli-grams	
Calories: 174 (160)*	Sodium: 174 milligrams	
Calories from fat: 90 (79)*	Carbohydrate: 17 grams	
	Dietary fiber: 1 gram	

* Figures in parentheses provide nutritional information if nuts are left out.

October

Columbus Day
Halloween

Columbus Day

October 12, observed the second Monday in October

On August 3, 1492, Christopher Columbus, an Italian, set sail from Spain on a voyage that changed the world forever. The common knowledge of the era said that the world was flat and that if you sailed beyond a certain point you would fall over the edge. A handful of scientists believed that the world was round. Columbus wanted to prove this theory and looked for money to finance an exploration of the seas. His native Italy, England, and Portugal all refused to support this "extreme" idea.

He finally convinced Queen Isabella of Spain to back his venture, because at the time trade merchants were looking for an easier route to Asia. (They believed they had to circumnavigate Africa and sail east.) Columbus proposed sailing west, to reach Asia by circling the globe. A condition of Queen Isabella's support was that Columbus also conquer some land for Spain. After many years of negotiating, he finally set sail on the *Santa María*, accompanied by the *Niña* and the *Pinta*. They landed in the New World on October 12, 1492.

For years Columbus was given credit for the discovery of the New World. Today controversy exists over whether he "discovered" a land that had been inhabited for years. We do know that he did bring this new land to the attention of the civilized world, which introduced Western civilization to this continent. His discovery initiated continuing contact between people of the Old World and the New. Over the years millions of people followed Columbus to the New World in search of freedom and a better life.

Although funded by Spain, Columbus was a son of Italy, and it was Italian Americans who began Columbus Day celebrations in America.

Congress passed a joint resolution in 1934 recognizing the achievements of Christopher Columbus. In 1968 an act of Congress was passed, requesting the president to proclaim the second Monday in October "Columbus Day."

Our Italian feast in honor of this day is a great menu for people with diabetes. Minestrone Soup is naturally low in fat, yet it's a powerhouse of nutrients. Soup is a great way to start a meal, because it is filling and makes it easier not to overeat when you get to the main course. Chicken Cacciatore is another low-fat winner. This tasty dish can be prepared a day ahead of time, which gives its flavors time to develop. The key here is to slightly undercook the chicken and to finish cooking it just before serving. The Almond Ricotta Cheesecake or the Chocolate Hazelnut Biscotti are a perfect way to top off this meal. The nutrition information provided for all these recipes helps you select the amount just right for you.

Columbus Day

Minestrone Soup

Chicken Cacciatore

Almond Ricotta Cheesecake

or

Chocolate Hazelnut Biscotti

Minestrone Soup

YIELD: 6 servings

½ cup white navy beans*
5 cups water
2 cloves garlic, minced
½ small onion, diced into small pieces
2 medium carrots, diced into small pieces
2 stalks celery, diced into small pieces
1 teaspoon basil

1 15-ounce can tomatoes, chopped, liquid included
1 cup zucchini, diced into small pieces
½ cup macaroni
1 cup spinach, cut into strips ½ inch wide by 1 inch long
6 teaspoons grated low-fat Parmesan cheese

Soak the navy beans overnight in 2 cups of cold water. Drain.

Place the beans in 3 cups water. Bring to a boil, reduce the heat, and simmer for 40 minutes, or until almost tender. Add the garlic, onion, car-

*You may substitute a 15-ounce can of cannellini beans, drained, for the dry navy beans and skip the cooking of the beans. Start with 2 cups water, the garlic, onions, carrots, celery, tomatoes, and basil. Simmer for 15 minutes and then add the canned beans when you add the zucchini and the pasta.

rots, celery, basil, and canned tomatoes and continue to simmer for 15 minutes. Add the zucchini and macaroni and cook for an additional 10 minutes. Add the spinach and turn off heat. Ladle into soup bowls and top with Parmesan cheese.

This soup should be thick with vegetables, beans, and pasta and could be a meal in itself for any occasion.

Serving size: ⅙ recipe	Total fat: 1 gram	Dietary fiber: 7 grams
Starch exchanges: 1	Saturated fat: 0 grams	Sugars: 7 grams
Vegetable exchanges: 2	Cholesterol: 0 milligrams	Protein: 7 grams
Calories: 135	Sodium: 270 milligrams	
Calories from fat: 10	Carbohydrate: 25 grams	

🐝

Chicken Cacciatore

YIELD: 4 servings

1 2-pound chicken, skin removed, cut into pieces, the legs and thighs separated, the breast cut into 4 equal pieces
1 medium onion, sliced
2 cloves garlic, finely minced
8 ounces mushrooms, quartered
2 stalks celery, sliced
½ medium green pepper, cut into strips
½ medium red pepper, cut into strips

1 15-ounce can tomatoes, diced, with juice
1 tablespoon tomato paste
¼ cup dry white wine
¼ cup Chicken Stock (see recipe, p. 21)
1 teaspoon basil
1 teaspoon oregano
⅔ cups raw rice (prepare according to package directions)

Preheat the oven to 350°.

Rinse the cut-up chicken under cold water and pat it dry with paper towels. Coat a large Dutch oven with cooking spray and set the pan over high heat. When the Dutch oven is hot, place the chicken inside and brown it on all sides. Remove the chicken and set it aside. Place the onion, garlic, mushrooms, celery, and peppers in the Dutch oven and sauté for 5 minutes. Turn the heat down to medium and add the tomatoes and tomato paste. Stir well. Return the chicken to the Dutch oven and stir. Add the wine, stock, and herbs. Bring to a boil. Cover and place in the oven. Bake for 30 minutes. Remove the cover from the Dutch oven, stir, and bake for an additional 20 minutes. Transfer the chicken to serving plates and cover with the vegetables and sauce that were cooked with the chicken. Serve with rice.

Serving size: ¼ recipe, ½ cup rice Starch exchanges: 2 Very-lean-meat exchanges: 3 Vegetable exchanges: 1	Calories: 312 Calories from fat: 45 Total fat: 5 grams Saturated fat: 1 gram Cholesterol: 79 milli-grams	Sodium: 578 milligrams* Carbohydrate: 36 grams Dietary fiber: 3 grams Sugars: 4 grams Protein: 30 grams

Almond Ricotta Cheesecake

YIELD: 1 8-inch cheesecake

½ cup graham cracker crumbs
¼ cup plus 1 tablespoon sliced almonds, toasted lightly and roughly chopped
2 tablespoons butter, melted
12 ounces low-fat cream cheese
½ cup Splenda (sugar substitute)

½ teaspoon almond extract
1 teaspoon vanilla extract
12 ounces low-fat ricotta cheese
¼ cup nonfat plain yogurt
2 tablespoons Amaretto liqueur (optional)
4 eggs

Preheat the oven to 300°.

Mix together thoroughly the crumbs, ¼ cup chopped almonds, and melted butter in a small bowl by hand. Press into an 8-inch round pan that has been sprayed with cooking spray. Place in the refrigerator to set while you prepare the filling.

In the bowl of an electric mixer fitted with the paddle attachment, combine the cream cheese, Splenda, almond extract, and vanilla. Beat until light and creamy. Scrape down the mixture from the sides of the bowl;

*This recipe is not recommended for low-sodium diets.

add the ricotta, yogurt, and Amaretto (if desired), mixing until smooth. Add the eggs one at a time, scraping down and mixing after each addition. Mix until smooth.

Pour the batter into the prepared pan. Sprinkle the remaining 1 tablespoon of almonds over the top of the cheesecake. Set the pan on a cookie sheet (with sides) and place in the oven. Fill the cookie sheet with water to provide a water bath for the cheesecake. Bake approximately 1 hour and 10 minutes. Check after 30 minutes, adding more water if needed. When the cheesecake is done, it will feel firm to the touch and a toothpick inserted into the center will come out clean. Allow it to cool at room temperature for 30 minutes and then in the refrigerator for at least 3 hours before removing it from the pan and serving.

To remove the cake from the pan, place the pan directly over low heat on the stove. Move it in a circular motion for 15 to 20 seconds. Place a plastic-wrap-covered plate over the pan. Press tightly and turn it over, tapping the bottom of the pan to release the cake. Place a serving plate against the bottom of the cake and turn it back over.

Serving size: ½₂ of cake	Calories from fat: 91	Carbohydrate: 8 (9)* grams
Starch exchanges: ½	Total fat: 10 grams	Dietary fiber: 1 gram
Medium-fat-meat exchanges: 1	Saturated fat: 5 grams	Sugars: 2 grams
Fat exchanges: 1	Cholesterol: 27 milligrams	Protein: 9 grams
Calories: 160 (168)*	Sodium: 180 milligrams	Alcohol: (1)* gram

*Figures in parentheses include the optional Amaretto.

Chocolate Hazelnut Biscotti

YIELD: 2 dozen biscotti

5 tablespoons butter, melted
5 tablespoons Splenda (sugar substitute)
2 eggs
1 teaspoon vanilla extract
1¼ cups bread flour

½ teaspoon baking powder
2 tablespoons cocoa powder
¼ cup mini chocolate chips
¼ cup chopped hazelnuts, lightly toasted

Preheat the oven to 350°.

Place the melted butter and Splenda in the bowl of an electric mixer fitted with the paddle attachment. Mix together until combined. Add the eggs and vanilla and mix together. Sift together the flour, baking powder, and cocoa and add them to the liquid ingredients. Add the chocolate chips and hazelnuts. Mix together to form a dough. Remove the dough from the bowl and place it on a lightly floured surface. Knead it together and roll it out into a cylinder 12 inches long. Place the cylinder on a cookie sheet that has been sprayed lightly with cooking spray. Flatten the dough with the palm of your hand to form a strip 2½ inches thick. Bake for 18 to 20 minutes, until set. Remove from the oven and cool. When the dough is cool, cut it into ½-inch slices and arrange them ½ inch apart on a cookie sheet. Rebake at 350° for 15 minutes, until crispy.

Serving size: 1 biscotti	Total fat: 4 grams	Carbohydrate: 7 grams
Starch exchanges: ½	Saturated fat: 2 grams	Dietary fiber: 0 grams
Fat exchanges: 1	Cholesterol: 25 milli-	Sugars: 1 gram
Calories: 75	grams	Protein: 2 grams
Calories from fat: 1	Sodium: 40 milligrams	

Halloween

October 31

alloween is a time for ghosts and goblins and trick-or-treating. Its roots date back to an ancient era before the time of Christ. The Celtic people in Ireland and Great Britain had a New Year's celebration called Samhain. They believed that the dead came back to earth searching for bodies to possess for the coming year. Not wanting to be possessed, the Celts dressed in costume and paraded noisily to scare away the spirits.

In the ninth century the Catholic Church proclaimed November 1 to be All Hallows' or All Saints' Day, a special time to honor the saints and pray for the dead. The name Halloween is derived from "All Hallows' Eve" because it is celebrated on the evening before All Saints' Day. Despite the efforts of the church to make this a solemn celebration, old ideas and the traditions of costumes and trick-or-treating prevailed. These customs migrated along with the Irish immigrants to the New World.

Trick-or-treating originated in Ireland as people would go door to door begging for food for a communal celebration. Legend tells us that if the villagers were generous, they would be blessed for the coming year. If they were stingy, bad things would happen to them. This later evolved to playing real tricks, such as writing on windows with soap and "greasing" doorknobs to make them difficult to open. A favorite trick in nineteenth-century New England was tipping over outhouses. Today, while costumes and treats are still a big part of the Halloween tradition, "tricks" have mainly died out.

If you have a party at your house for children or adults, get into the spirit by decorating. Greet guests with a wreath on your door. Start with an artificial Christmas wreath, spray it with black spray paint, and decorate it with inexpensive plastic skulls and crossbones. Tape up black and orange crepe paper, "spiderwebs," and "skeletons" around the house to add to the atmosphere. Put your emphasis on decor and games for the children. Make sure you have plenty of nutritious food on hand, and try to see that all the children have a balanced meal before they start on goodies.

Our "adult" menu can be modified for a children's party. Tomato Soup with Black Olive "Eyeballs" is a hit with any age. Offer miniature carrots and add rice to the chicken to round out the menu for the little ones. Instead of cutting the Pumpkin Brownies after baking, use a jack-o'-lantern stencil and sift powdered sugar on the sheet of brownies for a decorative touch.

Halloween

Tomato Soup with Black Olive "Eyeballs"
Spinach Salad with Apple Cider Vinaigrette
Drunken Chicken with Beet Sauce
Brussels Sprouts Nests
Pumpkin Brownies

or

Orange-Chocolate Chip Cookies

Tomato Soup with Black Olive "Eyeballs"

YIELD: 4 servings

1 15-ounce can low-sodium tomatoes
3 tablespoons tomato paste
¼ cup finely minced onion
1 stalk celery, finely minced
1 bay leaf
⅛ teaspoon thyme

3 cups water
1 teaspoon salt
1 teaspoon white pepper
3 tablespoons cornstarch mixed with
   3 tablespoons water
4 black olives, sliced into rings

In a 2-quart or larger pot, add all the ingredients except the cornstarch mixture and the black olives. Cook over medium heat, partially covered, for 30 minutes. Remove the bay leaf. Puree the soup in a blender and then strain it through a fine sieve. Return the soup to the pot and bring it back to a boil. Slowly add the cornstarch mixture to the soup while whisking, until the soup reaches the desired thickness. Turn the heat down and simmer the soup gently for 5 minutes. Add the sliced black olives. Remove from the heat and serve.

Serving size: ¼ recipe	Total fat: 1 grams	Carbohydrate: 16 grams
Starch exchanges: 1	Saturated fat: 0 grams	Dietary fiber: 2 grams
Calories: 74	Cholesterol: 0 milligrams	Sugars: 6 grams
Calories from fat: 7	Sodium: 673* milligrams	Protein: 2 grams

Spinach Salad with Apple Cider Vinaigrette

YIELD: 4 servings

Salad

1 large hard-boiled egg, shelled and dipped in blue or yellow food coloring, then chopped into small pieces
4 ounces spinach, stems removed and larger leaves torn in half
1 large apple, peeled and cut into fine strips

Juice of 1 lemon
8 ounces mushrooms, washed, sliced
½ cup jicama, peeled and cut into fine strips
¼ cup Apple Cider Vinaigrette (recipe follows)

Note: As soon as you prepare the apple, mix it with the lemon juice so the apple strips will stay white. Dyeing the egg gives the salad an unusual look for Halloween.

*This recipe is not recommended for low-sodium diets.

Place all the ingredients in a large bowl and toss with the Apple Cider Vinaigrette.

Serving size: ¼ recipe	Total fat: 8 grams	Carbohydrate: 10 grams
Vegetable exchanges: 2	Saturated fat: 1 gram	Dietary fiber: 5 grams
Fat exchanges: 1½	Cholesterol: 53 milli-	Sugars: 6 grams
Calories: 115	grams	Protein: 4 grams
Calories from fat: 69	Sodium: 74 milligrams	

Apple Cider Vinaigrette

YIELD: ½ cup

1 teaspoon Dijon mustard	3 tablespoons olive or canola oil
Pinch of salt	3 tablespoons water
Pinch of white pepper	1 teaspoon Splenda (sugar substitute)
2 tablespoons cider vinegar	

Combine all the ingredients and mix well. Cover and refrigerate. The vinaigrette will keep for 1 week.

Serving size: 1 table-	Total fat: 5 grams	Dietary fiber: 0 grams
spoon	Saturated fat: 1 gram	Sugars: 0 grams
Fat exchanges: 1	Cholesterol: 0 milligrams	Protein: 0 grams
Calories: 47	Sodium: 5 milligrams	
Calories from fat: 46	Carbohydrate: 0 grams	

Drunken Chicken with Beet Sauce

YIELD: 4 servings

Drunken Chicken

1 2-pound chicken, cut in half, skin removed
1 cup dry white wine*
½ cup Chicken Stock (see recipe, p. 21)
¼ cup rice vinegar
2 tablespoons rum or brandy*
1 green onion, chopped small
1 teaspoon ginger
1 teaspoon freshly ground black pepper
2 teaspoons garlic salt

Rinse the chicken under cold water and pat it dry with paper towels. Place it in a dish. In a separate bowl, combine the rest of the ingredients and pour over the chicken. Cover and let the chicken marinate for 12 to 24 hours in the refrigerator, turning occasionally.

Preheat the oven to 400°.

Remove the chicken from the marinade and place it in a roasting pan that has been coated with cooking spray. Roast for 35 to 40 minutes. When the chicken is done, the juices should run clear and the internal temperature at the thickest part should be 165°. Cut up the chicken and place the pieces in Brussels Sprouts Nests (recipe follows). Spoon Beet Sauce (recipe follows) over the chicken and serve.

Serving size: ¼ recipe	Total fat: 4 grams	Carbohydrate: 0 grams
Very-lean to lean-meat exchanges: 4	Saturated fat: 1 gram	Dietary fiber: 0 grams
	Cholesterol: 99 milli-	Sugars: 0 grams
Calories: 174	grams	Protein: 30 grams
Calories from fat: 38	Sodium: 231 milligrams	Alcohol: .7 grams

* The alcohol in the marinade contributes fewer than 5 calories and less than 1 gram of alcohol to the finished dish. You may substitute water if you do not want to use alcohol.

Beet Sauce

2 medium beets, washed, with the
    leafy green tops cut off
1 cup water
1 small potato, peeled and cut in
    quarters

½ teaspoon salt (optional)
¼ teaspoon white pepper
1 teaspoon rice vinegar

Simmer the beets and potato in the water, covered, for 60 minutes. Being careful not to break the skins, lift the beets out of the cooking water. Reserve this cooking water and put the beets into a dish of cold water for a few minutes. Put the potato in a blender or food processor. Remove the peel from the beets. This is most easily done by rubbing it off with your hands. Cut off the stems and then cut the beets into quarters. Place the beets in the blender with the potatoes, salt, pepper, and vinegar. Puree until smooth. Add a little of the cooking water to make an easily poured bright red sauce. Spoon this over the chicken.

Serving size: ¼ recipe	Saturated fat: 0 grams	Dietary fiber: 1 gram
Vegetable exchanges: 1	Cholesterol: 0 milligrams	Sugars: 2 grams
Calories: 23	Sodium: 315 (23)* milli-	Protein: 1 gram
Calories from fat: 0	grams	
Total fat: 0 grams	Carbohydrate: 5 grams	

🌿

Brussels Sprouts Nests

YIELD: 4 servings

4 large brussels sprouts
1 cup water

1 teaspoon Splenda (sugar substitute)

Cut the base of a brussels sprout about ¼ inch so the outer leaves fall off or are easily stripped off. Cut the base again and strip a few more leaves

*Figure in parentheses does not include salt.

until you reach the light green, tightly wrapped core. Repeat with the other 3 brussels sprouts. Set aside.

Cut the cores in half and slice them ¼ inch thick. Bring the water and Splenda to a boil. Add the sliced brussels sprouts and boil, covered, over medium-low heat for 3 minutes. Add the leaves and continue to cook for 2 minutes more. Drain and keep warm until ready to serve.

Divide the leaves into 4 equal portions. Arrange them on 4 serving plates, making a nest of the brussels sprouts. Place pieces of Drunken Chicken inside each nest and top with Beet Sauce.

Serving size: ½ cup	Total fat: 0 grams	Carbohydrate: 4 grams
Vegetable exchanges: 1	Saturated fat: 0 grams	Dietary fiber: 2 grams
Calories: 19	Cholesterol: 0 milligrams	Sugars: 0 grams
Calories from fat: 1	Sodium: 11 milligrams	Protein: 1 gram

Pumpkin Brownies

YIELD: 24 brownies

1 cup all-purpose flour
1 teaspoon baking powder
½ teaspoon baking soda
½ teaspoon pumpkin pie spice
¼ cup granulated sugar
½ cup brown sugar

4 teaspoons Equal (12 packets)
¼ cup vegetable oil
2 large eggs
1 cup Libby canned pumpkin
½ cup chopped walnuts (optional)

Preheat the oven to 350°.

Lightly spray a 9-by-13-inch baking pan with cooking spray. Combine the flour, baking powder, baking soda, and pumpkin pie spice in a small bowl. Set aside. Combine the sugars, Equal, oil, eggs, and pumpkin in a large bowl. Slowly stir the dry ingredients into the pumpkin mixture. Mix well. Stir in the chopped walnuts if using. Pour the batter into the prepared pan. Bake for approximately 20 minutes, or until a toothpick inserted in the center comes out clean. Cut into 24 equal-size pieces.

Serving size: 1 brownie	Total fat: 4 (3)* grams	Carbohydrate: 11 grams
Starch exchanges: 1	Saturated fat: 0 grams	Dietary fiber: 0 grams
Calories: 84 (70)*	Cholesterol: 18 milli-	Sugars: 5 grams
Calories from fat: 36	grams	Protein: 2 (1)* grams
(24)*	Sodium: 50 milligrams	

❧

Orange-Chocolate Chip Cookies

YIELD: 2½ dozen cookies

3 tablespoons Splenda (sugar substitute)
½ cup butter
1 egg
½ cup orange juice
1 teaspoon grated orange zest

1 cup all-purpose flour
½ teaspoon salt
1 teaspoon baking powder
½ cup chopped walnuts
½ cup raisins
½ cup chocolate chips

Preheat the oven to 350°.

In the bowl of an electric mixer fitted with the paddle attachment, beat together the Splenda and butter until light and creamy. Beat in the egg, juice, and zest. Sift together the flour, salt, and baking powder. Add to the mixer bowl along with the walnuts, raisins, and chocolate chips. Blend to combine completely but do not overmix. Drop by the tablespoonful† onto a cookie sheet coated with cooking spray and press down to make each cookie ½ inch thick. Bake for 15 to 16 minutes, or until lightly browned.

Serving size: 1 cookie	Total fat: 5 grams	Carbohydrate: 8 grams
Starch exchanges: ½	Saturated fat: 3 grams	Dietary fiber: 0 grams
Fat exchanges: 1	Cholesterol: 16 milli-	Sugars: 4 grams
Calories: 82	grams	Protein: 1 gram
Calories from fat: 48	Sodium: 88 milligrams	

*Figures in parentheses provide nutritional information if nuts are left out.
†Dip the spoon in flour when dropping cookies. This will keep the dough from sticking to the spoon.

November

Thanksgiving

Thanksgiving

*The fourth Thursday in November in the United States; the
second Monday in October in Canada*

C elebrating and giving thanks for a bountiful harvest and good for-
tune is a tradition that Europeans observed long before the early set-
tlers migrated to the New World. Farmers in Europe filled a curved
horn with grain and fruit—the original cornucopia or horn of plenty—and
gave thanks for the abundance of food and other blessings.

The Thanksgiving tradition in the United States dates back to 1621,
when about fifty Pilgrims and ninety Native Americans celebrated a communal feast together. The first Thanksgiving dinner included turkey and
probably other fowl such as ducks and geese, roasted on a spit. Fruits of
the harvest included pumpkins, squash, corn, and cranberries that grew
wild in the New England bogs. The Native Americans taught the Pilgrims
to grow and cook pumpkin and corn, thus helping them to survive in their
new homeland.

The first Thanksgiving in Canada took place in 1578, in Newfoundland. Martin Frobisher, an English navigator, held a formal ceremony to
give thanks for a safe journey. He was later immortalized when a bay in the
Atlantic Ocean off of Canada was named for him.

Nowadays Thanksgiving is an occasion during which we all can take
time to be thankful for our many blessings. For many people the day is
spent watching a football game followed by eating a big dinner. "Abundance" is the theme of the day when it comes to food, but fight the couch-
potato syndrome by making physical activity a part of your day. Go for a
run, a walk, or a bike ride before you settle down in front of the football
game.

One way to handle the immensity of the feast is to spread it out
throughout the day. Our menu is designed to let you do just that. You can

serve the Festive Relish Tray and Apricot and Walnut Loaf early in the day or during the football game. The soup, turkey, dressing, vegetable, and salad become the main meal. Save the pie for later in the evening. That way you can enjoy more variety without overdoing on any one aspect.

There are many tricks to reducing sugar, fat, and calories in this meal. The fresh cranberries used in the sauce are a perfect example. They are very low in calories and can be sweetened with Equal or Splenda. White-meat turkey is naturally low in fat. The Pumpkin Pie recipe is so good no one will believe it does not have added sugar! Don't forget to give thanks for the many improvements in food technology that have enabled us to make lower-calorie food taste so delicious and help people with diabetes maintain good glucose control and good health.

Thanksgiving

Festive Relish Tray with Dijon Pimiento Dip

Apricot and Walnut Loaf

Squash and Apple Soup in Acorn Squash Shells

Potato-Stuffed Roasted Turkey Breast

Turkey Gravy

Steamed Broccolini

Apple-Orange Cranberry Sauce

Pumpkin Pie with Whipped Topping

or

Chocolate Chiffon Cake with Spiced Topping

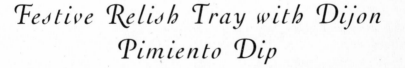

Festive Relish Tray with Dijon Pimiento Dip

Radish roses, scallion brushes, carrot curls, and red pepper stars will make a festive tray. They will take a little time and patience to perfect, however. The good thing is, if they don't turn out, you get to eat your mistakes!

YIELD: 12 servings

12 small radishes
1 bunch green onions
2 large carrots

12 long, thin red peppers
1 recipe Dijon Pimiento Dip

Radish Roses

Remove the root and the stem. Cut paper-thin slices in the 4 sides of the radish. Slice down from the stem to the root, curving the knife slightly as the cut is made to form a petal shape without cutting through completely. On top of the radish, with a sharp knife, carve out 3 V-shaped intersecting grooves to form a star. Place the radish in ice-cold water for at least 30 minutes when you are finished cutting. Repeat with all the radishes.

Green Onion Brushes

Cut off the root end and the green leafy sections, leaving a stalk 3 inches long. Cut lengthwise through the stalk to the center. Rotate the stalk a quarter turn and cut again lengthwise to the center. Repeat again. Put in ice-cold water for at least 30 minutes. Repeat this process with all the green onions.

Carrot Curls

Peel the carrots and slice them very thinly lengthwise. The thinner you slice them, the better the curl. Place the slices in a container of ice-cold water for at least 30 minutes.

Red Pepper Bursts

Cut off a third the length of each, keeping the two-thirds end with the stem. Make ¼-inch-wide cuts all the way down to the stem. Soak in ice-cold water for at least 30 minutes. If you cannot find long, thin peppers, cut regular sweet peppers into 4 pieces and then cut into narrow strips almost all the way to one end. Place the peppers in a container of ice-cold water.

Remove the vegetables from their water containers and arrange them attractively on a platter with the dip (recipe follows) in a small bowl in the center. Serve.

Serving size: ½12 of relish tray	Total fat: 0 grams	Dietary fiber: 1 gram
Vegetable exchanges: 1	Saturated fat: 0 grams	Sugars: 1 gram
Calories: 26	Cholesterol: 0 milligrams	Protein: 1 gram
Calories from fat: 1	Sodium: 9 milligrams	
	Carbohydrate: 6 grams	

Dijon Pimiento Dip

YIELD: 1¼ cups

1 cup plain yogurt
1 3-ounce jar pimientos, drained
1 teaspoon Dijon mustard

1 teaspoon lemon juice
Few drops of Tabasco sauce

Put all the ingredients into a blender or food processor and puree until smooth. Refrigerate until ready to use.

Serving size: 1 table- spoon	Total fat: 0 grams	Dietary fiber: 0 grams
	Saturated fat: 0 grams	Sugars: 1 gram
Free food	Cholesterol: 0 milligrams	Protein: 1 gram
Calories: 9	Sodium: 60 milligrams	
Calories from fat: 2	Carbohydrate: 1 gram	

Apricot and Walnut Loaf

YIELD: 1 loaf (9 by 5 by 3 inches)

2 cups all-purpose flour
¼ cup Splenda (sugar substitute)
1 tablespoon baking powder
2 teaspoons grated orange zest
1 cup orange juice
2 tablespoons canola oil

1 egg
¼ teaspoon cinnamon
1 cup chopped dried apricots (about
¼-inch pieces)
1 cup chopped walnuts

Preheat the oven to 350°.

Put the flour, Splenda, baking powder, and orange zest in the bowl of an electric mixer fitted with the paddle attachment. Mix until combined. Add the remaining ingredients and mix until completely combined. Do not overmix. Pour the batter into a loaf pan that has been coated with cooking spray. Bake for 45 to 50 minutes. When done, the loaf will be lightly browned and firm to the touch. Cool it on a rack at least 1 hour before slic-ing. Slice into 20 servings.

Serving size: 1 slice	Total fat: 5 grams	Carbohydrate: 15 grams
Starch exchanges: 1	Saturated fat: 0 grams	Dietary fiber: 1 gram
Fat exchanges: 1	Cholesterol: 11 milli-	Sugars: 4 grams
Calories: 115	grams	Protein: 3 grams
Calories from fat: 43	Sodium: 64 milligrams	

Squash and Apple Soup in Acorn Squash Shells

YIELD: 6 servings

3 round acorn squashes, softball size
2 teaspoons olive oil
2 tablespoons finely minced onion
1 pound butternut squash, peeled and cut into ½-inch cubes
1 medium potato, peeled and quar-tered

2 large apples, peeled, cored, and quartered
3 cups Chicken Stock (see recipe, p. 21)
1 bay leaf
⅛ teaspoon thyme
½ teaspoon Worcestershire sauce

Cut an acorn squash in half to form 2 cups. Scoop out the seeds and discard them. Repeat the process with the 2 remaining squashes. Bring 4 cups of water to a boil, add the squash halves, and cook for 15 minutes, covered. Remove the squash and let it cool.

Heat a 3-quart pot on medium-high heat. Add the olive oil and onion and cook for 2 minutes. Add the remaining ingredients. Bring to a boil. Scoop out most of the flesh from the cooked acorn squash halves, leaving ¼ inch of squash still attached to the sides and ¾ inch left in the bottom. Be careful not to put a hole in the squash, as they will function as your serving bowls. Add the scooped-out squash to the simmering soup. Cook for 5 minutes. Remove the bay leaf. Pour the soup into a blender or food processor. Cover. While holding the top down with a kitchen towel, blend on low speed for 1 minute. Turn up the speed and puree until smooth. Return the soup to the pot and bring it back to a boil. Check for taste. Add salt or white pepper to your liking. Trim a little off the bottom of the outside of the squashes so that they will stand level and then ladle the soup into acorn squash bowls.

Serving size: ⅙ recipe	Total fat: 3 grams	Carbohydrate: 34 grams
Starch exchanges: 2	Saturated fat: 0 grams	Dietary fiber: 5 grams
Calories: 156	Cholesterol: 0 milligrams	Sugars: 7 grams
Calories from fat: 23	Sodium: 271 milligrams	Protein: 3 grams

Potato-Stuffed Roasted Turkey Breast

YIELD: 12 servings

1 4–5-pound boneless turkey breast
1 recipe Potato Stuffing (recipe follows)
½ teaspoon salt
½ teaspoon freshly ground black pepper
1 teaspoon sage
½ teaspoon paprika

Rinse the turkey under cold water and pat it dry with paper towels. Butterfly the turkey breast by cutting lengthwise from one side of the breast to within 1 inch of the opposite side. Open the meat and lay it flat between 2 pieces of plastic wrap. With a meat mallet, pound the turkey to ½-inch thickness. Remove the top piece of plastic and evenly spread the Potato Stuffing from one end to 2 inches from the other end.* Roll up the roast, starting from the long end where the stuffing is, jelly-roll style. Tie the roast together in 2 or 3 places. Season it with the salt, pepper, sage, and paprika. Wrap it tightly in foil, seal the ends, and poach it in simmering water, covered, for about 40 minutes, or until the internal temperature reg-

* If you stuff the breast in this manner, the Potato Stuffing does not have to be baked as directed in the following recipe.

isters 150° on a meat thermometer. Remove the turkey from the water and let it rest for 15 minutes.

Preheat the oven to 425°.

Unwrap the turkey and carefully place it in a roasting pan that has been coated with cooking spray. Roast for 20 to 30 minutes to give the skin a light brown color. Let the turkey rest for 20 minutes. Cut the strings and, for a lower-fat roast, remove the skin just before slicing.

Serving size: ½ recipe, 4 ounces	Calories from fat: 13	Carbohydrate: 9 grams
Vegetable exchanges: 2	Total fat: 1 gram	Dietary fiber: 1 gram
Very-lean-meat exchanges: 5	Saturated fat: 0 grams	Sugars: 1 gram
Calories: 210	Cholesterol: 95 milli- grams	Protein: 38 grams
	Sodium: 239 milligrams	

Potato Stuffing

YIELD: 6 ½-cup servings

4 ounces turkey bacon, cut into ½-inch pieces
1 small onion, chopped small
1 clove garlic, minced
¼ cup celery, chopped small
2 medium potatoes, baked, cooled, and diced into ½-inch pieces
2 teaspoons chopped fresh rosemary

1 teaspoon chopped fresh thyme
¾ cup Chicken Stock (see recipe, p. 21)
1 cup bread crumbs
¼ cup chopped parsley
1 teaspoon freshly ground black pepper

Preheat the oven to 350°.

In a skillet over medium-high heat, cook the turkey bacon for about 2 minutes. Add the onion, garlic, and celery and cook for 5 minutes, stirring often. Remove the skillet from the heat and place the contents in a large bowl with the potatoes, herbs, stock, bread crumbs, parsley, and pepper.

Toss well. Either bake in a dish, covered, at 350° for 30 minutes or add as the stuffing to the turkey breast (see previous recipe).

Serving size: ⅙ recipe	Total fat: 2 grams	Carbohydrate: 16 grams
Starch exchanges: 1	Saturated fat: 0 grams	Dietary fiber: 1 gram
Calories: 98	Cholesterol: 7 milligrams	Sugars: 2 grams
Calories from fat: 20	Sodium: 267 milligrams	Protein: 3 grams

Steamed Broccolini

YIELD: 6 servings

12 ounces broccolini*   Pinch of salt and white pepper

Wash the broccolini and discard about 1 inch of the stem. Place the broccolini in a steamer basket and cook for about 5 to 6 minutes. When it is tender and looks dark green, season with salt and pepper. Serve.

Serving size: 2 ounces	Total fat: 0 grams	Carbohydrate: 1 gram
Free food	Saturated fat: 0 grams	Dietary fiber: 1 gram
Calories: 13	Cholesterol: 0 milligrams	Sugars: 1 gram
Calories from fat: 0	Sodium: 33 milligrams	Protein: 1 gram

*Broccolini, or baby broccoli, is a new hybrid vegetable. It is a cross between broccoli and Chinese kale and is also known as gai lan. Broccolini has long, slender stems similar to those of pencil asparagus and is topped with small buds with dark green leaves and mild green stalks.

Apple-Orange Cranberry Sauce

YIELD: 12 servings

1½ cups fresh or frozen cranberries
1 apple, peeled and shredded
1 orange, peeled, seeded, and diced
   small
1 teaspoon orange zest

Juice of 1 orange
½ cup Splenda (sugar substitute)
½ cup water
1 tablespoon cornstarch mixed with
   1 tablespoon water

In a small saucepan, combine all the ingredients except the cornstarch mixture. Bring to a boil, reduce the heat, and simmer, uncovered, for 4 to 5 minutes, or until the cranberry skins begin to pop open. Thicken the liquid with the cornstarch mixture and cook 2 minutes more. Remove the sauce from the heat, put it into a bowl, and refrigerate 2 to 3 hours, or until well chilled, before serving.

Serving size: ¼ cup	Total fat: 0 grams	Carbohydrate: 7 grams
Vegetable exchanges: 1*	Saturated fat: 0 grams	Dietary fiber: 1 gram
Calories: 24	Cholesterol: 0 milligrams	Sugars: 3 grams
Calories from fat: 0	Sodium: 4 milligrams	Protein: 0 grams

*Even though the main ingredients in this recipe are fruit, the carbohydrate content is closer to that found in a vegetable exchange.

Pumpkin Pie with Whipped Topping

YIELD: 1 9-inch pie, 10 servings

1 9-inch frozen deep-dish pie shell, prebaked
¾ cup Splenda (sugar substitute)
Pinch of salt
1 teaspoon pumpkin pie spice
1 teaspoon cinnamon
2 eggs

1 teaspoon vanilla extract
1 15-ounce can Libby pumpkin
1 12-ounce can nonfat evaporated milk
1¼ cups Cool Whip Lite whipped topping (optional)

Preheat the oven to 350°.

Combine the Splenda, salt, pumpkin pie spice, and cinnamon in a small mixing bowl. Set aside. Beat together the eggs and vanilla in a large mixing bowl. Beat the pumpkin into the eggs. Add dry ingredients and mix to completely combine. Gradually add in the evaporated milk. Mix to blend thoroughly. Place the pie shell on a cookie sheet and fill shell with the pumpkin mixture. Bake for 30 to 35 minutes. When done, the filling will feel firm to the touch. Cool, cut, and serve with topping if desired.

Serving size: ⅒ of pie	Total fat: 6 grams	Carbohydrate: 16 grams
Starch exchanges: 1	Saturated fat: 3 grams	Dietary fiber: 2 grams
Fat exchanges: 1	Cholesterol: 44 milli-	Sugars: 2 grams
Calories: 143	grams	Protein: 5 grams
Calories from fat: 57	Sodium: 150 milligrams	

Chocolate Chiffon Cake with Spiced Topping

YIELD: 1 5-by-9-inch loaf

1¾ cups cake flour
1¼ cups Splenda (sugar substitute)
2 teaspoons baking powder
½ teaspoon salt
½ cup unsweetened cocoa powder
¾ cup boiling water

½ cup canola oil
6 egg yolks
1 teaspoon vanilla extract
9 egg whites
1 teaspoon cream of tartar
½ cup mini chocolate chips

Preheat the oven to 325°.

Sift the flour, 1 cup of the Splenda, the baking powder, and salt into the mixing bowl of electric mixer. Make a well in the center. Mix together the cocoa and boiling water. Add the cocoa mixture to the center of the flour with the oil, egg yolks, and vanilla. Mix until completely combined, using the paddle attachment on an electric mixer.

In a separate bowl, whip the egg whites with cream of tartar and the remaining ¼ cup of Splenda until the mixture forms soft peaks. Fold the meringue gently into the flour mixture. Mix in thoroughly. Fold in the chocolate chips.

Pour the batter into a 5-by-9-by-4-inch loaf pan coated with cooking spray and bake for 50 minutes, or until a toothpick inserted in the center comes out clean. Serve with Spiced Topping.

Spiced Topping

1 teaspoon cinnamon
½ teaspoon nutmeg

1 cup Cool Whip Lite whipped topping

Stir the spices into the topping until completely combined. To serve, spoon onto a slice of cooled cake.

Serving size: 1½-inch slice	Calories from fat: 90	Sodium: 141 milligrams
Starch exchanges: 1	Total fat: 10 grams	Carbohydrate: 16 grams
Fat exchanges: 2	Saturated fat: 2 grams	Dietary fiber: 1 gram
Calories: 165	Cholesterol: 71 milligrams	Sugars: 3 grams
		Protein: 4 grams

December

Hanukkah
Las Posadas
Christmas
Kwanzaa

Hanukkah

An eight-day celebration beginning on the twenty-fifth of the Hebrew month of Kislev, this holiday falls on varying dates in December.

*H*anukkah, sometimes called the Feast of Lights, celebrates both a victory of the Jewish religion and freedom over tyranny. Many years ago a Syrian king named Antiochus ordered the Jewish people to reject their God. He forbade them to study the Torah (the whole body of Jewish literature), ravaged and defiled their temples, and ordered them to worship Greek gods.

Some of the Jews, led by Judah Maccabee, rebelled and refused to worship these gods. Judah and his brothers formed an army known as the Maccabees, which fought for three years and ultimately were successful in driving the Syrians out of Israel. They reclaimed the temple in Jerusalem, cleansed it of all the Greek symbols, and rededicated this holy place. When they searched for oil to light the N'er Tamid, or eternal light, which should never be extinguished, they found only enough to last one day. They lit the light and a miracle occurred: the one-day supply of oil lasted for eight days.

The celebration of Hanukkah lasts for eight days in memory of the miracle of the oil. Candles are lit and prayers are recited each night. A special candleholder called a menorah is used for the occasion. It holds nine candles in a straight line, eight of which must be the same height. The shamash—the candle used to ignite all the others—is a little higher than the other eight. Hanukkah is a happy time, and families celebrate at home. In addition to lighting the menorah, gifts (frequently of money), games, and special foods help to make this a festive occasion for everyone.

Our Hanukkah menu works well for people with diabetes and other health concerns. Both the soup and entrée are very low in fat and calories. They help to balance the higher-fat Potato and Pear Pancakes for an overall well-rounded meal. Adding a bowl of fresh fruit as a dessert alternative is a thoughtful gesture. Arrange the fruit in a clear glass bowl or basket to make an attractive addition to your table.

Potato Pancakes, or latkes, are a traditional Hanukkah food, especially appropriate because they are cooked in oil. They have simple and readily available ingredients. Preparation is easy with the help of a food processor; the key to success is to be sure to grate your potatoes and onions finely enough. These pancakes are not a make-ahead food; for the best taste they need to be eaten as soon as they are prepared. Be sure to serve them with applesauce—unsweetened, of course—and sour cream (the low-fat variety works fine). None of the other items on the menu require such last-minute attention. If you substitute foods for some of those we have suggested, keep preparation time in mind so you can have plenty of time to prepare your Potato Pancakes.

Hanukkah

Beet Borscht

Orange Roughy à la Orange

Potato and Pear Pancakes with Chunky Applesauce and
Sour Cream

Baked Butternut Squash

Zimsterne Cookies

Beet Borscht

YIELD: 6 servings

4 cups water
4 medium beets, peeled and cut into
    julienne (long, thin) strips
1 medium onion, finely diced
1½ cups shredded green cabbage
2 beef bouillon cubes

1 teaspoon freshly ground black
    pepper
1 bay leaf
1 cup low-sodium tomato sauce
1 tablespoon lemon juice
Fresh dill or parsley for garnish

Bring all the ingredients except the garnish to a boil in a 2-quart soup
pot and simmer for 30 minutes. Remove the bay leaf, ladle the soup into
bowls, and garnish with a sprig of dill or chopped fresh parsley.

Serving size: 8 ounces	Total fat: 0 grams	Carbohydrate: 10 grams
Vegetable exchanges: 2	Saturated fat: 0 grams	Dietary fiber: 3 grams
Calories: 49	Cholesterol: 0 milligrams	Sugars: 7 grams
Calories from fat: 3	Sodium: 345 milligrams*	Protein: 2 grams

*This recipe is not recommended for low-sodium diets.

Orange Roughy à la Orange

In this dish the roughy is steamed with vegetables and oranges for a unique adaptation of a classical dish.

YIELD: 4 servings

1½ pounds orange roughy, striped
  bass, or sole
1 teaspoon tarragon
2 oranges, 1 peeled and cut into 8
  slices
¼ cup thinly sliced zucchini

¼ cup very thinly sliced carrot
¼ cup thinly sliced yellow squash
½ teaspoon salt
4 teaspoons white wine
4 teaspoons water

Preheat the oven to 375°.

Lay out 4 sheets of aluminum foil, each 6 by 12 inches, and spray one side of each with cooking spray. Cut the fish into 4 equal pieces. Place a piece in the center of each foil sheet. Sprinkle each piece with ¼ teaspoon of the tarragon. Top each piece with 2 orange slices. Next divide the zucchini, carrot, and yellow squash equally over the fish. Squeeze the juice of the other orange over the vegetables and sprinkle the fish with the salt, white wine, and water. Fold the foil sheets to make 4 tight packages. Put these on a cookie sheet and bake for 25 minutes. When done, the fish will be white, flaky, and juicy. Take the packages out of the oven and be very careful of the hot steam that will escape when you unwrap them. Gently lift the fish off each sheet onto a dinner plate. Pour any liquid that remains in the foil over the fish.

Serving size: ¼ recipe, 1 piece of fish	Calories: 157	Sodium: 251 milligrams
	Calories from fat: 12	Carbohydrate: 9 grams
Vegetable exchanges: 2	Total fat: 1 gram	Dietary fiber: 2 grams
Very-lean-meat exchanges: 3	Saturated fat: 0 grams	Sugars: 7 grams
	Cholesterol: 0 milligrams	Protein: 26 grams

Potato and Pear Pancakes with Chunky Applesauce and Sour Cream

YIELD: 8 servings

Pancakes

½ cup peeled and grated pears
1 cup peeled and grated potato
2 teaspoons lemon juice
2 tablespoons matzo meal
2 tablespoons all-purpose flour
1 teaspoon salt (optional)

½ teaspoon white pepper
½ cup egg substitute
2 teaspoons canola oil
Chunky Applesauce (recipe follows)
Low-fat sour cream

Grate the pear and potato separately in a food processor or by hand. Mix the grated pear with the lemon juice. Add the potato and mix well. Blend in the matzo meal, flour, salt, and pepper. Then add the egg substitute and mix well.

Coat a nonstick fry pan with cooking spray, add the oil, and over medium heat drop approximately 2 tablespoons of batter onto the fry pan. Using the back of the spoon, form the batter into a round pancake. Repeat until all the batter is used. Cook for 6 to 8 minutes on each side, or until the pancakes are golden brown and cooked throughout. Serve with Chunky Applesauce or low-fat sour cream.

For pancakes only; does not include applesauce or sour cream

Serving size: 2 pancakes	Saturated fat: 0 grams	Dietary fiber: 1 gram
Starch exchanges: 1	Cholesterol: 0 milligrams	Sugars: 1 gram
Calories: 71	Sodium: 320 (24)* milli-	Protein: 3 grams
Calories from fat: 21	grams	
Total fat: 2 grams	Carbohydrate: 10 grams	

*Figure in parentheses does not include salt.

Chunky Applesauce

YIELD: 8 servings

4 medium McIntosh apples
2 tablespoons water

1 teaspoon cinnamon
1 tablespoon lemon juice

Peel the apples, cut them into quarters, and remove the cores. Cut each quarter into approximately 10 slices. Place all the ingredients into a 2-quart pot, cover, and cook for about 20 minutes over medium heat, stirring occasionally, until the apples are soft. Mash lightly. If you prefer smooth applesauce, puree it in a blender. Refrigerate the applesauce, covered, until ready for use. It will keep in the refrigerator for up to 3 days.

Serving size: ¼ cup	Total fat: 0 grams	Carbohydrate: 10 grams
Fruit exchanges: ½	Saturated fat: 0 grams	Dietary fiber: 1 gram
Calories: 38	Cholesterol: 0 milligrams	Sugars: 8 grams
Calories from fat: 0	Sodium: 0 milligrams	Protein: 0 grams

Zimsterne (Spiced Star) Cookies

YIELD: 3 dozen 2-inch stars

¼ cup butter
¼ cup honey
¼ cup Splenda (sugar substitute)
2 eggs
½ cup pineapple juice

3 cups all-purpose flour
1 teaspoon baking powder
1¼ teaspoons cinnamon
1 teaspoon nutmeg
½ teaspoon ginger

Preheat the oven to 375°.

In the bowl of an electric mixer fitted with the paddle attachment, beat together the butter, honey, and Splenda until the mixture is light and creamy. Beat in the eggs. Add the pineapple juice and mix in. In a separate bowl, sift together the flour, baking powder, cinnamon, nutmeg, and ginger. Add to the liquid mixture and mix until combined. Remove the dough from the bowl and place it on a lightly floured surface. Flatten it out to make an 8-inch square, wrap in plastic, and chill at least 1 hour.

Place the dough on a lightly floured surface and roll out to a ¼-inch thickness. Using a star-shaped cookie cutter, cut out stars and arrange them about ½ inch apart on a cookie sheet coated with cooking spray. Bake for 13 to 15 minutes, or until light golden brown.

Serving size: 1 cookie	Saturated fat: 0 grams	Dietary fiber: 0 grams
Starch exchanges: 1	Cholesterol: 15 milli-	Sugars: 3 grams
Calories: 65	grams	Protein: 1 gram
Calories from fat: 15	Sodium: 29 milligrams	
Total fat: 2 grams	Carbohydrate: 11 grams	

Las Posadas

December 16 through 24

*L*as posadas means "the inns" or "the shelters" in Spanish. A religious
and social celebration that takes place for nine nights, from December 16 to 24, the holiday known as Las Posadas commemorates
Joseph and Mary's journey to Bethlehem and their search for shelter prior
to the birth of Christ. Las Posadas is a reenactment of this difficult journey.
It is an elaborate preparation for La Navidad (Christmas) in Mexico and
some Central American countries

This tradition dates back to the sixteenth century and St. Ignatius Loy-
ola, who used an Aztec festival to teach about the birth of Christ. He also
wanted to replace the nine-day celebration of the birth of the Aztec Sun
god with a Christian celebration. What started as a novena, or nine days of
prayer, eventually moved from the church to the community and was celebrated in people's homes.

Las Posadas includes a procession led by children, followed by adults
and musicians. They travel to a different house in the village or neighbor-
hood each night looking for lodging. When they enter the designated
house, they begin the evening with prayer; soon after, the celebration begins, full of music, fireworks, food, candy, and treats for all. Children and
adults alike anticipate this joyous religious occasion.

In traditional homes and rural areas, particularly in the south of Mexico, La Navidad is still very much a religious holiday. However, just as the
Magi brought gifts to the infant baby Jesus, celebrants also bring toys to
good little girls and boys on January 6, the Day of the Kings. In the north-
ern parts of Mexico, especially those adjacent to the United States, Christmas trees and Santa Claus are the order of the day.

Our menu is appropriate for any night during Las Posadas or for La

Navidad. It is designed for a group, as Mexican customs and culture dictate. Some of the items are high in calories, so be sure to share them with lots of friends. Include some lower-calorie items so that your guests have lots of choices. Serving buffet style is considerate of any guests who have diabetes, as it lets each person easily determine the amount of food he or she wishes to eat.

If your family and friends live close by, encourage them to adopt the true spirit of Las Posadas and walk to your party. That way they will benefit from the physical activity that can help keep their blood glucose in the appropriate range. Or if walking isn't an option, play music so that everyone can dance, a very enjoyable way to stay active.

Las Posadas

Sopa de Albóndigas

Festival Salad

Vegetable Tamale Pie

Tijuana Chicken

Baked Mexican Lasagna

Warm Apple Empanadas

or

Fresh Fruit Quesadillas

or

Tapioca and Strawberry Parfait

Sopa de Albóndigas

YIELD: 12 servings

1 pound lean ground beef
½ cup cooked rice
2 tablespoons finely minced onion
1 teaspoon salt
1 teaspoon chili powder
¼ cup bread crumbs
1 egg
½ medium onion, sliced into strips

2 medium carrots, cut in half lengthwise, then sliced into half-moon shapes
1 stalk celery, sliced
½ small zucchini, sliced into strips
6 cups low-sodium Beef Stock (see recipe, p. 112)
1 tablespoon chopped fresh cilantro

Combine the beef, cooked rice, onion, salt, chili powder, bread crumbs, and egg. Mix well. Shape into 1-inch meatballs. Set aside. Bring all the remaining ingredients except the cilantro to a boil in a large pot. Add the meatballs when the stock begins to boil. Cover and reduce the heat to a simmer. Cook for 20 minutes. Skim off any fat that rises. Turn the heat off. Add the chopped cilantro and serve.

Serving size: 5⅓ ounces	Calories from fat: 70	Sodium: 289 milligrams
Vegetable exchanges: 1	Total fat: 8 grams	Carbohydrate: 6 grams
High-fat-meat	Saturated fat: 3 grams	Dietary fiber: 1 gram
exchanges: 1	Cholesterol: 44 milli-	Sugars: 1 gram
Calories: 139	grams	Protein: 11 grams

Festival Salad

YIELD: 12 servings

1 small head romaine lettuce
6 small beets, cooked, peeled, and
  sliced
2 oranges, peeled and sliced
2 apples, cored and thinly sliced
2 bananas, peeled and thinly sliced
½ small jicama, peeled, quartered,
  and thinly sliced

1 pineapple, peeled, cored, quartered, and thinly sliced
2 tablespoons lemon juice
1 tablespoon water
1 teaspoon Equal (3 packets)
Seeds of 1 pomegranate
1 lime, cut into small wedges
¼ cup chopped peanuts

Line a shallow serving bowl with the outer leaves of the romaine let-tuce. Shred the remaining lettuce and place the shreds on top of the leaves. Arrange the beets, oranges, apples, bananas, jicama, and pineapple in an eye-appealing pattern atop the lettuce. Mix together the lemon juice, water, and Equal. Drizzle this over the fruit. Garnish the salad with the pomegranate seeds, lime wedges, and chopped peanuts.

Serving size: ½ of recipe	Total fat: 2 grams	Carbohydrate: 17 grams
Starch exchanges: 1*	Saturated fat: 0 grams	Dietary fiber: 4 grams
Calories: 83	Cholesterol: 0 milligrams	Sugars: 10 grams
Calories from fat: 16	Sodium: 13 milligrams	Protein: 2 grams

🌿

Vegetable Tamale Pie

YIELD: 6 servings, a 9-inch square baking dish

Masa

1⅓ cups warm water
1 teaspoon salt
1½ cups cornmeal

½ cup masa flour
2 tablespoons butter
2 tablespoons egg substitute

Bring the water and salt to a boil, add the cornmeal, and simmer slowly, 10 minutes. Remove from the heat and add the masa flour. Mix well. Blend in the butter and egg substitute. Stir well. Cover and set aside.

Preheat the oven to 375°.

Filling

1 tablespoon canola oil
1 small onion, finely diced
1 clove garlic, minced
½ cup broccoli florets, cut small
½ cup green pepper, diced into small pieces
½ cup fresh tomatoes, diced

1 small jalapeño pepper, sliced (optional)
½ cup corn kernels
2 tablespoons black olives, sliced
1 cup water
1 teaspoon cumin
1 teaspoon chili powder

Heat the canola oil in a heavy skillet or saucepan. Lightly sauté the onion and garlic in the canola oil for 2 minutes. Add all the remaining in-

*Although the salad contains primarily fruit and vegetables, the addition of peanuts adds protein and fat and makes the nutrient profile similar to a 1-starch exchange.

gredients. Cover and simmer for 5 minutes. Coat a 9-inch-square baking dish with cooking spray. Spread a third of the masa mixture on the bottom of the baking dish. Spread the filling mixture evenly over it. Cover evenly with the remainder of the masa. Bake, covered, for 20 minutes. Remove the cover and continue to bake for another 20 minutes, or until lightly browned.

Serving size: ⅙ of recipe	Calories from fat: 79	Sodium: 498 milligrams*
Starch exchanges: 2	Total fat: 9 grams	Carbohydrate: 39 grams
Vegetable exchanges: 1	Saturated fat: 3 grams	Dietary fiber: 5 grams
Fat exchanges: 1	Cholesterol: 11 milli-	Sugars: 2 grams
Calories: 248	grams	Protein: 6 grams

Tijuana Chicken

YIELD: 6 servings

½ cup V-8 juice
2 stalks celery, thinly sliced
1 medium onion, peeled and thinly
    sliced

1 carrot, thinly sliced
1½ pounds skinless, boneless
    chicken breast, cut into 6 pieces
1 cup salsa (mild or hot)

Preheat the oven to 375°.

Coat a baking dish with cooking spray. Pour in the V-8 juice and add the celery, onion, and carrot. Place the chicken breasts on top. Spread the salsa over the chicken. Cover and bake for 45 minutes. When done, the chicken will be opaque inside, with a slight pink color from the V-8 juice and the salsa.

Serving size: ⅙ recipe, 4 ounces	Calories from fat: 13	Carbohydrate: 27 grams
Very-lean-meat exchanges: 3½	Total fat: 1 gram	Dietary fiber: 1 gram
	Saturated fat: 0 grams	Sugars: 3 grams
	Cholesterol: 65 milli-	Protein: 27 grams
Vegetable exchanges: 1	grams	
Calories: 148	Sodium: 219 milligrams	

*This recipe is not recommended for low-sodium diets.

Baked Mexican Lasagna

YIELD: 4 servings

½ pound lean ground turkey (skin-less)
1 tablespoon minced garlic
½ cup finely chopped onion
¼ cup finely chopped green pepper
2 tablespoons sliced black olives
¼ cup tomato paste

1 cup salsa (mild or hot, your choice)
4 6-inch flour tortillas
1 4-ounce can green chilies, drained and diced into ¼-inch pieces
½ cup shredded part-skim mozzarella cheese

Preheat the oven to 375°.

Cook the turkey, garlic, onion, and green pepper in a nonstick pan over medium heat, stirring to break up the meat. When the turkey is no longer pink and the pieces are small (about the size of a pea), add the olives, tomato paste, and salsa. Bring to a boil and remove from heat.

Spray a 6-inch square baking dish with cooking spray. Place 1 flour tortilla on the bottom and top it with a fourth of the turkey mixture, a fourth of the green chilies, and a fourth of the cheese. Repeat this process 3 more times with the other tortillas. Bake for 20 minutes, or until the lasagna is heated through. Remove it from the oven and let it rest 5 minutes before serving.

Note: This recipe could be easily doubled and baked in a 6-by-10-inch dish if you want to serve it to a larger group.

Serving size: ¼ recipe	Calories from fat: 90	Sodium: 451 milligrams*
Starch exchanges: 2	Total fat: 10 grams	Carbohydrate: 29 grams
Medium-fat-meat ex-changes: 2	Saturated fat: 3 grams	Dietary fiber: 3 grams
	Cholesterol: 53 milli-grams	Sugars: 2 grams
Calories: 274		Protein: 18 grams

*This recipe is not recommended for low-sodium diets.

Warm Apple Empanadas

YIELD: 12 empanadas

2 Granny Smith apples
½ teaspoon grated lemon zest
1½ tablespoons unsweetened apple
   juice
½ tablespoon lemon juice
2 tablespoons butter, chopped
⅛ teaspoon plus ⅓ teaspoon
   cinnamon

3 teaspoons Equal (9 packets)
½ cup unsweetened applesauce
1 chilled sugar-free pie dough
1 egg
1 tablespoon water

Preheat the oven to 350°.

Peel and quarter the apples. Remove the cores. Slice each quarter across the narrow side into thin slices, less than ⅛ inch thick. Place the apples, lemon zest, apple juice, lemon juice, and butter in a shallow fry pan over medium heat. Cook, stirring constantly, until the apples are soft, about 10 to 12 minutes. Remove from the heat. Add ⅛ teaspoon cinnamon, 1½ teaspoons Equal, and the applesauce, stirring to combine completely. Place in refrigerator to cool.

To assemble, roll out the pie dough ⅛ inch thick on a lightly floured surface. Using a cookie cutter, cut out dough circles 3½ inches in diameter. Take the dough scraps, work them together, reroll, and cut out as many circles as possible. You should get at least 12. Whisk together the egg and water to make an egg wash. Place 1 tablespoon of the apple mixture in the center of each dough circle. Use a pastry brush to lightly brush the egg wash around the edge of half of each circle of dough, about ⅓ inch from the edge. Fold the dough over the filling so that the edges meet and press with your fingers to seal.

Arrange the empanadas 1 inch apart on a nonstick cookie sheet that has been coated with cooking spray. Lightly brush the tops with egg wash. Combine the other 1½ teaspoons Equal and ⅓ teaspoon cinnamon. Sprinkle this evenly over the egg-washed empanadas. Bake 15 to 17 minutes, or until lightly browned. Remove the empanadas from the oven and let them sit 5 minutes before serving.

They can be served as finger food or on a dessert plate with low-fat vanilla ice cream.

Serving size: 1 empanada	Calories from fat: 65	Sodium: 76 milligrams
	Total fat: 7 grams	Carbohydrate: 16 grams
Starch exchanges: 1	Saturated fat: 4 grams	Dietary fiber: 1 gram
Fat exchanges: 1	Cholesterol: 52 milli-	Sugars: 4 grams
Calories: 137	grams	Protein: 3 grams

Fresh Fruit Quesadillas

YIELD: 8 servings

½ cup light sour cream
¼ teaspoon vanilla extract
⅛ teaspoon Equal (½ packet)
1 mango, peeled and diced into ½-inch pieces
1 pint fresh strawberries, cleaned and sliced into quarters

1 small D'Anjou pear, cored and diced into ¼-inch pieces
1¼ tablespoons honey
1 tablespoon finely chopped fresh mint
1 cup shredded light jack cheese
4 8-inch low-fat flour tortillas

Mix together the sour cream, vanilla, and Equal. Place in the refrigerator to chill. Place the prepared fruits in a bowl. Warm the honey slightly in the microwave. Stir together the honey and chopped mint and toss gently with the fruit. Lay out the tortillas and distribute half the cheese on half of each tortilla. Strain any excess liquid from the fruit. Divide the fruit over the cheese-covered halves of tortillas and top with the remaining cheese. Fold each tortilla closed. Coat a skillet with cooking spray and preheat it over medium heat. Grill each quesadilla on both sides until golden brown. Cut each in half and serve with the sweetened sour cream.

Serving size: ½ Quesadilla	Calories: 234	Sodium: 383 milligrams*
	Calories from fat: 73	Carbohydrate: 36 grams
Starch exchanges: 1	Total fat: 8 grams	Dietary fiber: 2 grams
Fruit exchanges: 1	Saturated fat: 4 grams	Sugars: 11 grams
High-fat-meat exchanges: 1	Cholesterol: 21 milli-grams	Protein: 7 grams

*This recipe is not recommended for low-sodium diets.

Tapioca and Strawberry Parfait

YIELD: 6 servings

3½ cups 2% milk
1 egg
2 tablespoons plus 1 teaspoon
   minute tapioca
1½ teaspoons Equal (4½ packets)

2 teaspoons vanilla extract
1 pint strawberries
½ cup Cool Whip Lite whipped
   topping

Bring 3 cups of the milk to a boil in a heavy saucepan. Mix together the remaining ½ cup milk, the egg, and tapioca. Add this to the hot milk while stirring with a wire whisk. Reduce the heat to a slow simmer and cook for 5 minutes, stirring occasionally. Remove the mixture from the heat and stir in the Equal and vanilla. Cool for 30 minutes in the refrigerator before proceeding. Clean the strawberries. Reserve 3 strawberries for garnish, and cut those in half. Slice the remaining berries. Divide half the sliced strawberries into the bottoms of 6 parfait or small white-wine glasses. Add a layer of the cooled pudding to each, using ½ of the mixture. Repeat with a layer of strawberries and another layer of pudding. Top each glass with the whipped topping and half a strawberry.

Serving size: 1 parfait	Total fat: 4 grams	Carbohydrate: 16 grams
Low-fat milk	Saturated fat: 3 grams	Dietary fiber: 1 gram
exchanges: 1	Cholesterol: 46 milli-	Sugars: 10 grams
Calories: 131	grams	Protein: 6 grams
Calories from fat: 40	Sodium: 82 milligrams	

Christmas

December 25

C hristians have celebrated Christmas, which commemorates the birth of Christ, since the fourth century. It is unclear how the December 25 date was chosen for this celebration, although it may have been a Christian attempt to counteract pagan celebrations held at this time. December 25 also heralds the beginning of the winter solstice, which may have been selected because this is the time when days begin to lengthen and Christians believe that Christ is the "true light of the world."

The age-old custom of gift-giving on this day was adopted from the Romans. Over the centuries the Germans and the Celts added such traditions as Yule logs, fir trees, decorative greenery, lights, and fires. In more recent times Christmas has taken on a more commercial tone. Shopping for this holiday has become a marathon event, and many businesses depend on the season for a successful year.

Santa Claus, a symbol of good cheer and holiday giving, is found in many parts of the world. His name may change from country to country, but his tradition of bringing gifts to children is a constant. Whether he is known as Santa Claus in the United States, St. Nicholas in the Czech Republic, Père Noël in France, or Julenisse in the Scandinavian countries, children everywhere look forward to the coming of this fat, jolly old man.

The music of the season is a crucial part of religious services and concerts; "caroling" is a Christmas institution. According to *Webster's,* to carol is "to celebrate in song." Legend says that caroling started with the angels when they announced the birth of Jesus in Bethlehem. People with the holiday spirit continue to join one another in song and perform for their neighbors during the Christmas season. Sometimes the performances are literally door-to-door, as neighbors serenade neighbors, or they may take a more formal appearance in churches, concert halls, or malls. Carols include all-time favorites such as Handel's "Joy to the World" and, more recently, Irving Berlin's "White Christmas." If you have a piano or other musical instrument and someone who can play it, caroling around the Christmas tree or fireplace is a nostalgic (and calorie-free!) way to celebrate.

Celebrating with food is an integral aspect of this season. Many practices date back thousands of years. If you or one of your loved ones has diabetes, do not despair. The first and most important thing to do is to figure out what holiday foods you really enjoy and then figure out how much of them you can include in your celebrations. If you really do not like a food, include something you really do like and don't waste calories on the other foods. Our Christmas menu gives you ideas on how to incorporate traditional foods without overdoing it.

Christmas

Orange Eggnog

Butternut Squash Soup

Cranberry Almond Green Salad

Christmas Crudités Wreath

Roast Rib of Beef with Whole Roasted Potatoes

Raspberry and Burgundy Pears with Sweetened Sour Cream

or

Red and Green Christmas Cookies

Orange Eggnog

YIELD: 8 6-ounce glasses

1 orange, peeled and sectioned
1 quart skim milk
12 ounces egg substitute

½ cup orange juice concentrate
½ cup Splenda (sugar substitute)

Cut out the white membrane from between the orange sections and remove any seeds. Place the sections in a blender with the remaining ingredients and puree until smooth.

Serving size: 6 ounces	Total fat: 2 grams	Carbohydrate: 16 grams
Nonfat milk exchanges: 1	Saturated fat: 0 grams	Dietary fiber: 0 grams
Calories: 120	Cholesterol: 3 milligrams	Sugars: 13 grams
Calories from fat: 14	Sodium: 140 milligrams	Protein: 10 grams

Butternut Squash Soup

YIELD: 5 cups

2 tablespoons finely chopped onion
2 teaspoons olive oil
1½ pounds butternut squash (weight before peeling), peeled, cut in half, seeds removed, and chopped into pieces no larger than ½ inch
1 cup sweet potato* diced into small pieces

1 15-ounce can low-sodium Chicken Stock (or see recipe, p. 21)
2 cups water
1 bay leaf
⅛ teaspoon white pepper
⅛ teaspoon thyme
½ teaspoon Worcestershire sauce
3–4 drops Tabasco sauce

Sauté the onion with the olive oil over medium heat in a 2- to 3-quart pot for 2 minutes. Add the squash, sweet potato, and all the remaining ingredients. Bring to a boil. Turn the heat down to medium-low. Cover and simmer slowly for 35 minutes. Check that the squash is fully cooked and soft. Remove the bay leaf. Pour the ingredients into a blender and cover. While holding down the top with a kitchen towel (so you do not get burned), blend on low speed for 1 minute. Turn the speed up one notch and blend for 10 seconds more. The soup should be smooth and golden orange in color.

Serving size: 5 ounces	Total fat: 1 gram	Carbohydrate: 13 grams
Starch exchanges: 1	Saturated fat: 0 grams	Dietary fiber: 2 grams
Calories: 64	Cholesterol: 0 milligrams	Sugars: 0 grams
Calories from fat: 12	Sodium: 106 milligrams	Protein: 2 grams

* Sweet potatoes have light brown skin and ivory flesh. Yams have reddish-brown skin with orange flesh.

Cranberry Almond Green Salad

YIELD: 4 servings

½ pound baby lettuce mix
2 pears, peeled and cut into julienne
   (long, thin) pieces
Juice of 1 lemon
½ cup Craisins (dried cranberries)

¼ cup sliced, toasted almonds
½ cup Lemon Vinaigrette (see
   recipe, p. 54) or Creamy Lemon
   Dressing (recipe follows)

Wash the greens and pat them dry gently with paper towels. Coat the pears with the lemon juice and add to the greens, along with the Craisins and almonds. Toss with the Lemon Vinaigrette or Creamy Lemon Dressing.

Creamy Lemon Dressing

¼ cup plain nonfat yogurt
2 teaspoons Dijon mustard
1 teaspoon Splenda (sugar substitute)

Juice of 1 lemon
1 tablespoon water
1 lemon, peeled and the fruit diced small

Blend all the ingredients together. Cover and refrigerate. Will keep refrigerated for 2 days.

Includes Creamy Lemon Dressing

Serving size: ¼ recipe	Total fat: 4 grams	Dietary fiber: 5 grams
Fruit exchanges: 2	Saturated fat: 0 grams	Sugars: 22 grams
Fat exchanges: 1	Cholesterol: 0 milligrams	Protein: 4 grams
Calories: 168	Sodium: 29 milligrams	
Calories from fat: 40	Carbohydrate: 32 grams	

Christmas Crudités Wreath

YIELD: 12–16 servings

2 large zucchini
2 large yellow squash
3 medium carrots, peeled
3 stalks celery
1 large red pepper, cut in half, seeds
    removed
1 large green pepper, cut in half,
    seeds removed

1 bunch broccoli, all but 2 inches of
    stem trimmed off
1 head red leaf lettuce, washed
1 cup Dijon Pimiento Dip (see
    recipe, p. 187)
1 pint small cherry or grape tomatoes
20 tiny radishes, both ends trimmed
2 tablespoons chopped fresh parsley

Wash all the vegetables. Using a melon baller, scoop out the flesh of the zucchini and yellow squash. Cut the carrots, celery, red pepper, and green pepper into strips approximately 1½ inches long by ¼ inch wide. Cut the broccoli into small florets. Line a large platter with the red leaf lettuce. Put a small dish of dip in the center of the platter. Arrange the vegetables, including the tomatoes and radishes, in groups around platter, alternating shapes and colors. Sprinkle the chopped parsley over the finished platter.

Does not include Dijon Pimento Dip

Serving size: ¾ cup vegetables	Total fat: 0 grams	Dietary fiber: 3 grams
Vegetable exchanges: 1	Saturated fat: 0 grams	Sugars: 3 grams
Calories: 32	Cholesterol: 0 milligrams	Protein: 2 grams
Calories from fat: 3	Sodium: 24 milligrams	
	Carbohydrate: 7 grams	

Roast Rib of Beef with Whole Roasted Potatoes

YIELD: 6–8 servings

Roast Rib of Beef

1 medium onion, roughly chopped
1 medium carrot, roughly chopped
2 stalks celery, roughly chopped
4 cloves garlic, cut in half
1 bay leaf
4½ pounds boneless rib roast (sometimes called rib eye) *or* 6½ pounds bone-in rib roast (sometimes called prime rib)
2 teaspoons kosher salt (optional)

2 teaspoons freshly ground black pepper
1 teaspoon dried thyme *or* 2 tablespoons fresh thyme
Whole Roasted Potatoes (recipe follows)
¼ cup dry red wine (optional)
2½ cups water
1 tablespoon tomato paste

Preheat the oven to 250°.

Lightly coat the bottom of a large roasting pan with cooking spray. Lay all the vegetables and the bay leaf flat in the pan. Rinse the roast and pat it dry with paper towels. Rub it with the salt, pepper, and thyme. Place the roast on the vegetable bed, add the Whole Roasted Potatoes if you desire, and cook in the oven, uncovered, until the meat is done to your liking (2 to 4 hours). Start checking for doneness at 2 hours by inserting the tip of a meat thermometer into the very center of the roast. Rare: 120°; medium rare: 128°; medium: 135°; medium well 145°; well done: 155°. When the roast is done to your liking, remove it from the pan and wrap it loosely in foil. Set it aside for at least 20 minutes before carving.

Set aside the potatoes and keep warm. Scrape together all the vegetables and any browned particles stuck to the bottom of the roasting pan and place them in a 2-quart pot. Pour any remaining liquid from the roast into a fat separator or skim off as much fat as possible. Add it, along with the wine, water, and tomato paste, to the pot. Boil over medium-high heat for 10 minutes. Strain and discard the vegetables. Return the "jus"—the strained, skimmed liquid—to the pot and continue to reduce it to about 1½ cups. Skim and discard all the fat that comes to the surface with a spoon or ladle. Thinly slice the roast and serve it with the jus.

Note: A whole rib roast is 7 bones long and weighs anywhere from 12 pounds boneless to 24 pounds bone-in. The larger end is near the shoulder and will have more fat inside the eye. The loin end will be smaller and leaner and is the more healthful choice.

Serving size: 4 ounces	Saturated fat: 6 grams	Dietary fiber: 0 grams
Medium-fat-meat ex-	Cholesterol: 89 milli-	Sugars: 0 grams
changes: 4	grams	Protein: 31 grams
Calories: 286	Sodium: 378 (83)* milli-	
Calories from fat: 144	grams	
Total fat: 16 grams	Carbohydrate: 2 grams	

Whole Roasted Potatoes

YIELD: 6 servings

6 small (3½ ounces each) round red potatoes, washed
1 tablespoon olive oil

2 teaspoons paprika
1 teaspoon garlic powder
½ teaspoon salt (optional)

Mix all the ingredients well so the potatoes are thoroughly coated. Arrange the potatoes around the rib roast on top of the vegetables. Roast the potatoes along with the rib roast. When the roast is done, set the potatoes aside to keep warm while you finish making the jus. If the potatoes are not tender or crisp enough for your taste, put them back into the roasting pan after all the vegetables have been scraped out. Increase the heat to 350° and return the pan to the oven. The potatoes should have a firm feel on the outside, and the center should seem tender when the tip of a knife is inserted. (If you would like to roast these potatoes by themselves for another occasion, roast them in a small pan at 400° for approximately 45 minutes, depending on size.)

Serving size: 1 potato	Saturated fat: 0 grams	Dietary fiber: 2 grams
Starch exchanges: 1	Cholesterol: 0 milligrams	Sugars: 0 grams
Calories: 102	Sodium: 200 (6)* milli-	Protein: 2 grams
Calories from fat: 22	grams	
Total fat: 2 grams	Carbohydrate: 19 grams	

*Figures in parentheses do not include salt.

Raspberry and Burgundy Pears with Sweetened Sour Cream

YIELD: 6 servings

½ cup low-fat sour cream
¼ teaspoon vanilla extract
1 tablespoon Equal (10 packets)
2 cups individually quick frozen
   raspberries
Juice of half a lemon

1 cup burgundy wine (or grape juice)
½ cup water
1 cinnamon stick
3 pears, preferably D'Anjou
6 fresh mint leaves

Mix the sour cream, vanilla, and ⅛ teaspoon Equal very well. Cover and refrigerate.

Combine the raspberries, lemon juice, and wine in a saucepan over medium heat. Cook 5 to 7 minutes, stirring constantly, totally breaking up the raspberries. Remove from the heat. Strain the mixture through a fine sieve, pushing through as much sauce and pulp as possible. Only seeds should remain. Discard the seeds.

Return the raspberry mixture to the pan, adding the water, cinnamon stick, and remaining Equal. Stir until the Equal is completely dissolved. Cook over very low heat, barely simmering.

Peel the pears, cut them in half, and carefully remove the cores with a small knife. Place the pears cut side down in a pan with the raspberry sauce. Be sure they all lay flat.

Using a spoon, baste the tops of the pears with the warm liquid. Simmer over very low heat for approximately 15 minutes on this side, basting the tops 5 more times while cooking.

Turn the pears over and simmer on this side for 15 minutes while basting the exposed tops 5 more times. Remove the pan from the heat. Let stand 5 minutes. Baste again.

Place pear halves on individual dessert plates, cut sides up.

Return the liquid to the heat and boil, stirring, 3 minutes to reduce the sauce. Discard the cinnamon stick. Remove the pan from the heat. Evenly distribute the sauce around each pear half.

Place 1 tablespoon of the sweetened sour cream in the cavity of each pear half and add a mint leaf. Serve immediately.

Note: This could be prepared before dinner up to the point at which the pears are removed from the stove. When you are ready to serve dessert, return the pan to low heat for 3 or 4 minutes to rewarm the pears. Then proceed as in the instructions.

Serving size: ⅙ of recipe	Saturated fat: 1 gram	Dietary fiber: 3 grams
Fruit exchanges: 1½ (2)*	Cholesterol: 6 milligrams	Sugars: 14 grams
Calories: 122 (130)*	Sodium: 8 milligrams	Protein: 1 gram
Calories from fat: 21	Carbohydrate: 22 (27)*	Alcohol: 2 (0)* grams
Total fat: 2 grams	grams	

* Figures in parenthesis indicate grape juice substituted for the wine.

Red and Green Christmas Cookies

YIELD: 3 dozen cookies

¼ cup canola oil
3 tablespoons Splenda (sugar substitute)
1 egg
1 teaspoon vanilla extract
½ cup crushed pineapple, drained
1 cup all-purpose flour
2 teaspoons baking powder

½ teaspoon baking soda
1 teaspoon cinnamon
½ cup oats
½ cup raisins
¼ cup green glazed maraschino cherries
¼ cup red glazed maraschino cherries

Preheat the oven to 325°.

Put the oil and Splenda in the bowl of an electric mixer. Mix until the Splenda is dissolved. Add the egg and vanilla; mix thoroughly. Add the crushed pineapple and mix until combined. In a separate bowl, sift together the flour, baking powder, baking soda, and cinnamon. Add to the mixer bowl along with the oats, raisins, and green and red cherries. Mix in just to combine. Scoop out the dough by tablespoonfuls onto a nonstick cookie sheet. Bake approximately 10 minutes. When done, the cookies will be a light golden color and soft in the center.

Serving size: 2 cookies	Saturated fat: 0 grams	Dietary fiber: 1 gram
Starch exchanges: 1	Cholesterol: 12 milligrams	Sugars: 4 grams
Calories: 84		Protein: 1 gram
Calories from fat: 32	Sodium: 83 milligrams	
Total fat: 4 grams	Carbohydrate: 12 grams	

Kwanzaa

December 26 to January 1

K wanzaa is an African American holiday that was established in 1966. It is an occasion for the African American people to gather in commemoration of their history and culture. It is also a special time to honor ancestors. It is not a religious celebration, but a celebration of heritage, pride, community, family, and culture. Kwanzaa is based on activities commonly held at traditional African "first fruit" celebrations: gathering of family, friends, and community; reverence for creation and the creator; commemoration of the past; commitment to high ideals; and celebration of the "good of life."

Each day one of the Nguzo Saba, or seven principles, that collectively provide a value system is stressed. The seven principles are these:

Umoja (oo-MO-jah)—Unity
Kugichagulia (koo-jee-cha-goo-LEE-ah)—Self-determination
Ujima (oo-JEE-mah)—Collective work and responsibility
Ujamma (oo-JAH-mah)—Cooperative economics
Nia (NEE-ah)—Purpose
Kuumba (koo-OOM-bah)—Creativity
Imani (ee-MAH-nee)—Faith

The seven symbols are:

Mkeka (mm-KEH-kah)—A straw mat representing tradition and history. (*Note:* All the other symbols that follow are placed on this mat.)
Kinara (kee-NAH-rah)—A candle holder symbolizing Africa and ancestors.

Mazao (mah-ZAH-oh)—Fruits and vegetables, symbolizing the results of collective labor.

Muhindi (moo-HIN-dee)—Ears of corn, symbolizing offspring. One is placed on the mat for each child in the family.

Kikombe cha umoja (kee-KOH-beh chah oo-MOH-jah)—A communal cup, symbolizing unity.

Zawadi (Zah-WAH-dee)—Gifts, usually handmade, which serve as a reward for promises kept during the previous year.

Mishumaa saba (mee-SHOO-mah SAH-bah)—The candles that represent the seven principles of Kwanzaa.

Unfortunately, the incidence of diabetes is high in African Americans, and it increases with age. Although traditional African American food plays an important role in this celebration, the principles of Kwanzaa make it essential that you honor your ancestors by serving food that will promote good health. Our recipes will help you to prepare favorites—even Sweet Potato Custard Pie—with fewer calories, less sugar, and less fat. The nutritional information provided, along with the principle of self-determination, can dictate portion size.

Kwanzaa

Tomato Rice Soup with Fennel

Grilled Pepper Salad with Balsamic Glaze

Slow-Roasted Short Ribs

Baked Greens

Pumpkin Cornbread

Sweet Potato Custard Pie

or

Southern Banana Pudding

Tomato Rice Soup with Fennel

YIELD: 6 servings

1 tablespoon canola oil
1 small onion, finely diced
¼ cup finely diced celery
1 large fennel bulb, finely diced
1 clove garlic, minced
1 tablespoon tomato paste
1 16-ounce can tomatoes, diced,
  with juice

4 cups low-sodium Vegetable Stock
  (see recipe, p. 11)
¼ cup white rice, raw
½ teaspoon white pepper
½ teaspoon dried dill

Over medium heat, using a 2-quart pot, heat the canola oil. Add the onion, celery, fennel, and garlic, and sauté for 5 minutes. Do not brown. Add the tomato paste. Stir well. Add the remaining ingredients, reserving the dill for garnish. Bring to a boil. Reduce the heat and simmer for 30 minutes. Check the seasoning and adjust for taste. Ladle the soup into warm bowls and top with the dill.

Serving size: 8 ounces	Total fat: 3 grams	Carbohydrate: 14 grams
Starch exchanges: 1	Saturated fat: 0 grams	Dietary fiber: 2 grams
Calories: 89	Cholesterol: 0 milligrams	Sugars: 1 gram
Calories from fat: 26	Sodium: 357 milligrams*	Protein: 2 grams

Grilled Pepper Salad with Balsamic Glaze

YIELD: 6 servings

Balsamic Glaze

1 teaspoon canola oil
1 tablespoon finely minced shallot
1¼ cups balsamic vinegar

2 tablespoons Splenda (sugar substitute)

In a small saucepan, heat the canola oil and sauté the shallot for 2 to 3 minutes. Add the balsamic vinegar and Splenda. Reduce the heat and simmer until the liquid reduces to about ½ cup and is "syrupy." Remove the pan from the heat and let the glaze cool to room temperature. Store it refrigerated in a covered container for up to 1 week.

Salad

1 medium red pepper
1 medium green pepper
1 medium yellow pepper
1 small head red leaf lettuce
1 small head romaine lettuce
1 tablespoon fresh lemon juice

1 tablespoon water
1 tablespoon olive oil
Dash of freshly ground black pepper
1 medium red onion, thinly sliced
    and separated into rings

*This recipe is not recommended for low-sodium diets.

Preheat the broiler.

Place the whole peppers on an oven rack and char them, turning them often until they turn black. Place the peppers in a paper bag, seal, and let them sit for 15 minutes. With a sharp knife, peel off the skin and any remaining black specks. Rinse the peppers with cold water if necessary and pat them dry. Cut them in half, remove the tops and all seeds. Cut each half into 3 long strips.

Wash the lettuce and dry the leaves well. Line 6 salad plates with the red leaf lettuce. Cut the romaine into ½-inch squares and mound these on top of red leaf. Mix the lemon juice, water, olive oil, and pepper and drizzle this over the lettuce. Arrange 1 strip of each color pepper on the lettuce. Place a few onion rings over the peppers. Dip a serving spoon into the Balsamic Glaze and drizzle a fine line of glaze over the top of the finished salads. You now have a colorful salad with a few wild black lines from the Balsamic Glaze—the colors of Kwanzaa!

Serving size: 1 salad	Total fat: 3 grams	Dietary fiber: 2 grams
Vegetable exchanges: 1	Saturated fat: 0 grams	Sugars: 5 grams
Fat exchanges: ½	Cholesterol: 0 milligrams	Protein: 2 grams
Calories: 55	Sodium: 5 milligrams	
Calories from fat: 24	Carbohydrate: 7 grams	

Slow-Roasted Short Ribs

YIELD: 6 servings

4 pounds beef short ribs, lean
1 large onion, diced into ½-inch
  pieces
2 medium carrots, diced into ½-inch
  pieces
4 stalks celery, diced into ½-inch
  pieces
2 cloves garlic, diced small
2 tablespoons tomato paste
2 tablespoons flour

½ cup dry red wine
3 cups water
1 teaspoon thyme
2 bay leaves
1 tablespoon Worcestershire sauce
½ teaspoon Tabasco sauce
¼ teaspoon salt
½ teaspoon freshly ground black
  pepper

Preheat the oven to 325°.

Trim the short ribs of any excess fat and season them with salt and black pepper.

In a large Dutch oven over medium heat, brown the short ribs on all sides. When they are done, take out the ribs and reserve them. Add the vegetables and sauté for 5 minutes or until they are lightly browned. Add the tomato paste. Stirring well, mix in the flour and continue to cook for 3 minutes. Add the remaining ingredients. Bring to a boil while continuing to stir. Return the meat to the Dutch oven. Cover and roast in the oven for 2 hours. Skim off any fat that has risen to the top. Remove the bay leaves. Serve with the vegetables that were cooked with the ribs and top with the cooking liquid. Small boiled potatoes would be an appropriate side dish served with this entrée.

Serving size: ⅙ recipe	Total fat: 12 grams	Carbohydrate: 10 grams
Lean-meat exchanges: 4	Saturated fat: 5 grams	Dietary fiber: 2 grams
Vegetables exchanges: 2	Cholesterol: 64 milli-	Sugars: 3 grams
Calories: 265	grams	Protein: 29 grams
Calories from fat: 104	Sodium: 271 milligrams	

Baked Greens

YIELD: 6 servings

1½ pounds greens—turnip, mustard, collard, or kale

6 strips turkey bacon, cut into strips ½ inch wide

1 medium onion, cut in half, then sliced

¼ cup cider vinegar

½ teaspoon salt

1½ cups boiling water

Preheat the oven to 375°.

Wash the greens several times to clean them thoroughly. Discard any tough stems and discolored leaves. Cut the leaves into strips ¾ inch wide. Heat a large Dutch oven and sauté the bacon with the onion for 5 minutes on medium-high heat. Add the greens, vinegar, salt, and boiling water. Mix well, cover, and bake for 30 minutes, or until the greens are tender.

Serving size: ⅙ recipe	Total fat: 3 grams	Carbohydrate: 8 grams
Vegetable exchanges: 1	Saturated fat: 1 gram	Dietary fiber: 4 grams
Lean-meat exchanges: 1	Cholesterol: 10 milli-	Sugars: 1 gram
Calories: 68	grams	Protein: 5 grams
Calories from fat: 24	Sodium: 213 milligrams	

Pumpkin Cornbread

YIELD: 1 12-by-8-by-2-inch bread

1¼ cups cornmeal
1⅓ cups all-purpose flour
½ cup Splenda (sugar substitute)
1½ tablespoons baking powder
1 teaspoon salt
1 teaspoon pumpkin pie spice
1 teaspoon cinnamon

1⅓ cups low-fat sour cream
½ cup 2% milk
6 eggs
8 tablespoons butter, melted
1 16-ounce can Libby pumpkin
¼ cup shelled pumpkin seeds (optional)

Preheat the oven to 350°.

Place the cornmeal, flour, Splenda, baking powder, salt, pumpkin pie spice, and cinnamon in a mixing bowl. Mix until completely combined. Add the sour cream and milk and mix until just combined. In a separate bowl, beat the eggs. Then add them to the cornmeal mixture with the melted butter. Mix lightly, scraping down the sides of the bowl. Add the pumpkin and mix until completely combined. Pour the batter into a 12-by-8-by-2-inch baking dish that has been coated with cooking spray. Coarsely chop the pumpkin seeds, if using, and sprinkle them over the top. Bake for approximately 45 minutes. When done, the bread will be a light golden color and feel firm to the touch. Cool it in the pan on a rack. Cut into 24 pieces and serve.

Serving size: 1 piece	Total fat: 8 grams	Carbohydrate: 16 grams
Starch exchanges: 1	Saturated fat: 4 grams	Dietary fiber: 1 gram
Fat exchanges: 1½	Cholesterol: 70 milligrams	Sugars: 1 gram
Calories: 149		Protein: 4 grams
Calories from fat: 72	Sodium: 355 milligrams*	

*This recipe is not recommended for low-sodium diets.

Sweet Potato Custard Pie

YIELD: 1 9-inch deep-dish pie

1 9-inch frozen deep-dish pie shell
1 15-ounce can sweet potatoes,
    drained
½ cup Splenda (sugar substitute)
Pinch of salt
¼ teaspoon nutmeg
½ teaspoon cinnamon

1 teaspoon vanilla extract
2 eggs
1 12-ounce can low-fat evaporated
    milk
1 cup Cool Whip Lite whipped top-
    ping
Cinnamon for garnish

Preheat the oven to 375°.

Prebake the frozen pie shell for approximately 8 to 10 minutes, until it is a light golden brown. Set it aside to cool. Reduce the oven temperature to 350°. Place the drained sweet potatoes in the bowl of an electric mixer fitted with the whisk attachment and mix on medium speed for about 2 minutes to break up the sweet potatoes. Add the Splenda, salt, nutmeg, cinnamon, and vanilla and continue to mix. Scrape the mixture down occasionally until potatoes are mashed.

In a separate bowl, whisk the eggs, add the evaporated milk, and mix them together thoroughly. Gradually add the egg mixture to the sweet potato mixture while mixing on medium speed, scraping down the sides of the bowl as you go. Mix thoroughly. Set the prebaked pie shell on a cookie sheet and carefully fill with the mixture. Place the cookie sheet with the pie on it in the preheated oven. Bake approximately 45 to 50 minutes. When done, the custard filling will feel firm to the touch. Cool the pie before serving. Top each slice with 2 tablespoons of the whipped topping and sprinkle lightly with cinnamon.

Serving size: ⅛ pie	Total fat: 10 grams	Carbohydrate: 32 grams
Starch exchanges: 2	Saturated fat: 3 grams	Dietary fiber: 1 gram
Fat exchanges: 2	Cholesterol: 55 milli-	Sugars: 3 grams
Calories: 252	grams	Protein: 7 grams
Calories from fat: 92	Sodium: 247 milligrams	

Southern Banana Pudding

YIELD: 6 cups

4 cups 1% milk
Pinch of salt
⅓ cup cornstarch
2 eggs
1 egg yolk
2 tablespoons butter, chopped

1 tablespoon plus 1 teaspoon Equal
 (14 packets)
2 teaspoons vanilla extract
8 ounces vanilla wafers
4 medium bananas

Place 3½ cups of the milk and the salt in a heavy saucepan over medium heat. Dissolve the cornstarch in the remaining ½ cup milk, add the eggs and yolk, and whisk to combine completely. Bring the milk on the stove to a boil. Whisk ½ cup of the hot milk into the cornstarch mixture, then whisk the cornstarch mixture back into the boiling milk. Stir constantly. Reduce the heat to a slow boil and cook for 2 minutes, still stirring constantly. The mixture will thicken. Remove it from the heat. Stir in the chopped butter, Equal, and vanilla extract. Stir to combine completely.

Assemble the pudding immediately in an 8-by-11-by-2-inch pan, while the mixture is hot. Arrange a third of the vanilla wafers evenly spaced over the bottom of the pan. Peel and slice all the bananas about ¼ inch thick. Place half the banana slices among the cookies. Spoon on half the custard mixture. Make a second layer with a third of the cookies and the remaining banana slices. Spoon on the remaining custard, smoothing it out evenly. Top with the remaining cookies. Cover with plastic wrap, pressing the wrap onto the custard around the cookies so that it does not develop a skin. Allow to set at least 4 hours before serving. Serve at the table by spooning into chilled bowls.

Serving size: ½ cup	Total fat: 9 grams	Carbohydrate: 30 grams
Starch exchanges: 2	Saturated fat: 3 grams	Dietary fiber: 1 gram
Fat exchanges: 1	Cholesterol: 62 milli-	Sugars: 15 grams
Calories: 217	grams	Protein: 5 grams
Calories from fat: 77	Sodium: 159 milligrams	

Index

noodles:
  lo mein stir-fry, Chinese greens and, 27
  veal marengo, 138
nopalitos salad, 80
nutmeg spiced topping, chocolate chiffon
      cake with, 194
nuts, *see specific types of nuts*

oats:
  apple crisp, 17
  cookies, red and green Christmas, 224
  sun-dried cherry and pineapple bar,
      152–53
olive "eyeballs," tomato soup with black,
      174–75
onions:
  lentils and rice with caramelized,
      158–59
  relish tray with Dijon pimiento dip,
      185–87
  vegetable kabobs, 126
orange roughy:
  á la orange, 200
  seafood frittata, 90
  Veracruz, 81
orange(s):
  cheesecake, Easter, 59–60
  -chocolate chip cookies, 180
  cranberry sauce, apple-, 192
  eggnog, 216
  orange roughy á la, 200
  salad, festival, 207–208

pancakes with chunky applesauce and sour
      cream, pear and potato, 201–202
parfait:
  Kahlúa, 84–85
  mint, 48
  strawberry:
    chiffon, 60–61
    tapioca and, 213
    yogurt, 94
  tapioca and strawberry, 213
Parmesan:
  broccoli, 37–38
  tomatoes, grilled, 101
parsnips and carrots, dilled, 69
Passover, 62–71
  about, 62–63
  brisket with horseradish sauce, tomato-
      garlic, 67–68

gefilte fish, 64–65
honey cake, 71
matzo ball soup, 66
menu, 64
parsnips and carrots, dilled, 69
potato kugel, 68–69
recipes, 64–71
tchatchouka, 70
pasta:
  lo mein noodle stir-fry, Chinese greens
      and, 27
  minestrone soup, 167–68
  salad, all-American, 146–47
peach cobbler, blueberry and, 151–52
peanut butter and banana cupcake surprise
      (filled with chocolate ice cream),
      135–36
pear(s):
  cranberry almond green salad, 218
  and potato pancakes with chunky
      applesauce and sour cream,
      201–202
  quesadillas, fresh fruit, 212
  raspberry and burgundy, with sweetened
      sour cream, 222–23
peas:
  black-eyed, good luck, 14–15
  split pea soup, 45
pecans:
  chicken fingers, 133–34
  wild rice, 37
peppers:
  green, *see* green pepper(s)
  red, red pepper(s)
  yellow pepper for grilled pepper salad
      with balsamic glaze, 228–29
pie(s):
  chocolate cream, 140
  coconut custard, 116
  pumpkin, with whipped topping,
      193
  sweet potato custard, 233
  vegetable tamale, 208–209
pimiento dip, Dijon, 187
  festive relish tray with, 185–87
pineapple:
  bar, sun-dried cherry and, 152–53
  carrot tzimmes, 159
  icing, vanilla, 162
    carrot cake with, 161–62
  salad, festival, 207–208

About the Authors

Carolyn Leontos, M.S., R.D., C.D.E., is a registered dietitian, a certified diabetes educator, and a tenured professor at the University of Nevada. She has counseled people on their diets and health for thirty years. The author of *What to Eat When You Get Diabetes: Easy and Appetizing Ways to Make Healthful Changes in Your Diet,* she has published many articles on both diabetes and nutrition in magazines and professional journals.

Debra Mitchell, Certified Executive Pastry Chef, is executive pastry chef at Treasure Island, a Mirage/MGM Hotel and Casino in Las Vegas, Nevada. She has won many medals in culinary competitions, including two "Best of Shows" in Las Vegas Culinary Salons. She previously worked in Atlantic City, New Jersey, at Trump Casino.

Kenneth Weicker, Certified Executive Chef, is executive chef of the Suncoast, a Coast Resorts Hotel and Casino in Las Vegas. In Atlantic City, New Jersey, he opened the Golden Nugget as executive sous-chef and later became executive chef for Trump Castle. Appointed executive chef of the Mirage in 1989, he most recently was executive chef of Treasure Island and was named Las Vegas's "Chef of the Year" in 1996.